What people a
Angels and Demons

"You'll be in for some surprises in this well-written, well-researched and informative look at angels by Ron Wenzel. A good read on an interesting topic."
Shirley Frazier, Angel Study Participant in Rosewood Heights, IL

"Angels are a fascinating subject that truly captivates those attending Wenzel's classes. Ron provides solid Biblical teaching about everything you want to know about angels. Many in our church have expressed interest in obtaining his new book that will provide even more insight to those wanting deeper knowledge about angels."
David Blackburn, Associate Pastor at Faith Fellowship Church in Alton, IL

"Very informative. In some very practical ways it helped me de-mystify the subject."
Mike Solomon, Youth Pastor at Godfrey First United Methodist Church in Godfrey, IL

"This year we had Ron Wenzel deliver a series of messages entitled Angels, Demons and the Unseen World. *Here are a few samples of what our people had to say: "I completely enjoyed this week. It changed my life." "Thank you so much for this excellent work!" "Really, REALLY enjoyed this series," "Very thought provoking! SO many new thoughts! I will not look at the topic of angels in the same way again!" "Eye-opening!" This feedback clearly demonstrates that people are interested in this topic and are drawn to Ron's engaging personality and excellent communication skills. I would certainly commend Ron and this series of lessons to anyone as a means to open eyes to the importance of these matters."*
Pastor Joel Lohr, Bethel Baptist Church in Kane, IL

Angels, Demons and
the Unseen World

Mary Kate Dannahirt
Ryan —
God bless you
and my angels watch
over you!

Ron Wh
10/5/15

Angels, Demons and the Unseen World

RON WENZEL

ISBN-13: 9780989843317
ISBN-10: 0989843319
Library of Congress Control Number: 2015911907
Madleigh Publishing House, Alton, IL

Acknowledgements

Obviously, God gets primary credit, but my wife **Carolyn** always comes next.
She has been lovingly supporting my antics for over 35 years.

This particular book is dedicated to a pair of Jacks:

Dr. Jack Acree

Dr. Jack Collins

I am grateful for their instruction in Bible College (Baptist) and seminary (Presbyterian).
I have valued them friends as well as mentors.
Dr. Acree is with the angels now, far too soon. The influence of both of these men will resonate for years to come with their many students and the people those students serve.

About the cover:

The artistry of my daughter-in-law, **Ashley Kopp Wenzel**, has captured the essence of the story told by this book. It blends several images beautifully; that's her gift. You can view more of her wonderful work at **www.ashleykopp.com**.

The primary scene is that of the angel Gabriel announcing the birth of Christ to Mary. This is the center of God's plan for the salvation of mankind. It is taken from a photo of a stained glass window at St. Ambrose Catholic Church in Godfrey, Illinois, where my mother and many of my friends worship.

The face of Satan, who works constantly to disrupt God's plan, is taken from a photo of the doorway of SS Peter and Paul School in Alton, Illinois. I attended this school while growing up, and always wondered why the face was there. (In the Middle Ages, it was thought that strategically placed gargoyles scared off demons; it continued as a tradition in some religious buildings long after that.)

In the background is the hand of God stretching to touch the hand of Adam, as beautifully depicted within the Sistine Chapel. God is still reaching out to every human being through His Son, Jesus Christ.

Illustrations within the book are classic paintings, mostly from the Renaissance, all in the public domain. In order of appearance, the artists are Caravaggio, Cranuch, Van Valckenborgh, Rembrandt, Titian, Reni, Feretti, Titian (again), Cibot and Sanzio.

Contents

Important: Before We Begin

IN ORDER TO get the most value from this book, the following information will be very helpful. The first section of each chapter provides a piece of the saga of the angels. The story portion of the chapter is in bold print, to distinguish it from the commentary that follows. Each story blends Scripture verses from various locations within the Bible, and fills in the story with speculative details to help the narrative flow smoothly. (This is especially true in the first two chapters.) The purpose of this structure is to enable the reader to grasp the story of the angels with understanding similar to that of a first century Jewish Christian.

Within the story, some sentences are italicized; these are actual Scripture verses that are incorporated into the narrative. Footnotes appear frequently to guide the reader toward portions of the Bible that contain or support the story being told. The second section (commentary) of each chapter gives further details, explanations and supporting information for that piece of the story.

Some readers will just want to do a "quick read" of the story of the angels, and that can be done easily by ignoring the footnotes. Those who crave more detail and understanding are advised to have this book in one hand and the Bible in the other. The reader that follows the rabbit trails that the footnotes present will find that the exercise will not only deepen their appreciation for the story of the angels, but also for the wonder of the Bible as a whole.

The story you are about to read is true. Like any story, it operates under some assumptions, some presuppositions. Before you read it, it would be helpful for you to know what some of them are:

- The words contained in the Bible are very close to those used by the original authors. We are reading a translation of those original words, but there are a number of excellent translations available (KJV, NKJV, NASB, etc.) and there is no significant disagreement among them. Thousands of ancient manuscripts and fragments firmly establish the accuracy of today's Bible.
- The original authors of the books of the Bible are the men traditionally identified as such. In other words, the apostle John wrote the gospel and letters that bear his name and the book of Revelation. Moses wrote the first five books of the Bible. Isaiah contains the words of Isaiah, etc. Some authors remain unknown.
- All the history contained in the Bible (Creation, the Flood, Abraham, the sagas of the kings of Israel and the early church, etc.) actually happened as described.
- God guided the process of selecting the 66 books that we call our Bible. Each of these books deserve inclusion, and no other books are worthy of being added.

To some folks reading this book, stating the above is stating the obvious. To others, these assumptions might seem outrageous. This book does not attempt to reconcile the Bible's content with today's culture. Rather, the intention is to help the reader view the story the Bible tells from the viewpoint of the authors and their original, ancient readers. The focus is not on what the modern reader believes, but what a first century Jewish Christian believed. These were the people who wrote the New Testament; they were also the intended audience of those gospels and letters. Before we can truly understand what Scripture means to *us*, we need to understand what it meant to *them*.

This leads us to two theological terms that will be useful to understand:

- Isogesis - bringing modern or outside thought into the Bible. Searching for ways to make the Bible say what you want it to say instead of what it actually says.
- Exegesis - drawing the actual meaning out of the words of Scripture.

As you probably guessed, our objective is to practice exegesis, to draw the story of the angels out of the Bible accurately. If this story is new to you, your initial reaction may be to dismiss it, and to replace what the Bible says with your own preconceived ideas. Take heart: the story of the angels builds as it goes along, and as more puzzle pieces fall into place it will be easier to digest.

In practicing exegesis, theologians employ a skill called *hermeneutics*, which is the practice of learning and understanding the customs that were in vogue at the time the Scripture was originally written. In order to build an understanding of the worldview of people in ancient Israel, this book occasionally draws upon ancient religious writings outside the Bible. We do not give such material equal weight to Scripture, of course; but we can better understand the mindset of the Bible's authors, and their original audiences, by becoming familiar with some of these writings. We need to think more like people who lived 2000-3000 years ago to better understand the story of the angels. This is a challenge, but an interesting one.

Many of the images and ideas we have today about angels do not originate in the Bible, but spring from literature and art from the Middle Ages. Works like *Paradise Lost* by Milton and Dante's *Inferno* are beautiful and amazing works of fiction that have made a huge impact on our cultural understanding of heaven, hell, angels and demons for centuries. However, it is important to remember they are *fiction*. Works of art and fiction from the Middle

Ages draw some factual information from Scripture and make some logical assumptions about the unseen spiritual world, but some *draw more upon each other than they do upon the Bible.*

What does this mean to you, the reader? It means a great deal of information in this book will be new to you, and that material will contradict much of what you think you know about angels, both good and evil.

It is generally recognized that the Bible tells the story of mankind's interaction with the God of Israel. Angels, both good and evil, are not merely "bit players" in the Biblical drama; they do not appear on a random basis. Angels are intimately involved in the events that shape human history. Their story has a beginning, a history and an end even as the saga of human beings does. It, too, is within the Bible: it's just a little harder to see.

Prologue

O, Hear the Angel Voices!

I T SEEMS MOST people don't think about angels often; when they do, it is probably around Christmas time. "Fall on your knees; o hear the angel voices" is a wonderful line from a favorite Christmas Carol. While it is true that angel voices indeed filled the air above Bethlehem on the night Jesus was born, it is by no means the only time that angel voices have been heard. The Bible teaches that all the angels sang for joy as God created the earth. Their voices must be magnificent; the apostle Paul implies that love itself is one of the few things more wonderful than the language the angels speak.

Angels, as originally designed by God, are first and foremost *messengers*. Their very name (in the original Greek and Hebrew terms) *means* messenger. Throughout history, the voices of angels, both good and evil, have had a tremendous impact on human history. Careful study of the Bible reveals a story about angels, nestled within the story of men, women and God. The epic struggle among angels and men rarely takes center stage, but it is completely intertwined with the cosmic story that the Bible tells. If the Bible is literally true, then angels have played an instrumental role in the most important events in human history and have far more impact on our lives today than we realize.

At the beginning of time, Adam and Eve heard the voice of Satan, the most powerful fallen angel, in the Garden of Eden. The voice of an angel prevented Abraham from sacrificing his son. Angels repeatedly appeared and spoke to Abraham's grandson, Jacob. Jacob saw angels ascending and descending on a ladder (or stairway to heaven), and they guarded him on his journeys. Jacob even wrestled with an angel on the night before his reunion with his brother Esau, an encounter he had feared for years. Angels administered plagues in Egypt and delivered the Ten Commandments on Mt. Sinai. When Moses died, Satan battled Michael the Archangel for his remains. Elsewhere in the Old Testament, angels announced the birth of Samson, emboldened Gideon, afflicted Job, spoke prophecy to Daniel.

At the center of history, the angel Gabriel told Mary of Nazareth she would give birth to the Messiah; not long after that, angel voices repeatedly spoke to Joseph in his dreams. Jesus heard soothing angel voices when He completed His fast in the desert, after He resisted the dark voice of Satan. Angel voices again spoke comfort the night before Christ was crucified when He anxiously sweat blood in the Garden of Gethsemane. Angels were at the tomb the day Jesus rose from the dead and they spoke to Mary Magdalene when she found the tomb empty.

When Jesus ascended to heaven, angels reminded His disciples of their Master's instructions. An angel spoke to Simon Peter while he was in prison and sentenced to death; the angel miraculously freed him from his chains and led him to safety. Many years later, while exiled on the island of Patmos, John the Apostle had fantastic visions of many angels who sang and worshipped in the throne room of God. As a result, John wrote the Book of Revelation, which tells the story of Christ's return. Within it, John tells how the voices of angels will thunder in the heavens, even as they wield fire, lightning and the elements of the weather during the earth's last days.

The Bible portrays angels as having been extremely powerful in the past and it also tells of the great power and influence they will hold in the future. From a Biblical standpoint, angels are active in human history today, just as they were at the dawn of time and just as they will be at the end of time. In our modern world of reason and science, the idea that angels impact our lives today is hard to accept. However, Scripture asserts this is the case, and if the Bible is an accurate picture of our reality, then angels are nearly as prominent upon the landscape of our times as human beings are.

Their story began at the beginning of time. It continues to unfold even now, and it continues into eternity.

Let's explore it.

1

In the Beginning

THE STORY BEGAN.

"I think...I think, therefore I am." The being that would one day be known as Satan winked into existence and was immediately aware of his surroundings in the heavens. *"Of course you are, My bright little star!"* replied the Lord. The angel was impressed by the power in that voice, but was perhaps even more enthralled with his newly-created self.

The angel would have blinked, but his eyes were not physical. He marveled at himself, living fire suspended in darkness. Intangible stones of every color imaginable, beyond imagination itself, gleamed upon and within him.[1]

Another, lesser angel, hovering nearby in the heavens, spoke admiringly. "You are like a son of the dawn."[2]

1　Ezekiel 28:13
2　Isaiah 14:12

"Yes," he said. "I am Lucifer." He basked for a moment in the admiration of the smaller flame.

"Take care, guardian Cherub[3]," said the Lord. *"We have fashioned you for purposes beyond yourself."* At this, Lucifer flickered involuntarily.

Lucifer strained to see the Lord. He sensed immense power, perhaps beyond measure, behind His voice. Then the Lord spoke a Word beyond comprehension and the darkness heaved and bent and a glint of light appeared far away, in the darkness. With a thought, Lucifer moved across the heavens to rest beside the new light. He glanced down at yet another being much like himself, though not so bright or beautiful.

"I think," said the new light.

"Perhaps," said Lucifer.

Another Word thundered silently, and a myriad of lights dotted the seemingly infinite darkness. Lucifer was pleased that all were lesser angels. Perhaps save one. He focused his attention on one whose splendor annoyed him.

"He is Michael," said another angel that was near him in the heavens. Deep within Lucifer the seed of the first rivalry took root.

Gradually, as the great variety of spiritual beings became aware, a low hum began to build among the angels and fill the void.

Lucifer was startled to realize that the very depth of his being vibrated in tune with the humming. The vibration was swelling within him so intensely that he feared he might burst. Before him, the darkness was swirling and dancing in a symphony of circular chaos, with clouds of

3 Ezekiel 28:14

substance beginning to take shape and form. The song of the angels filled the heavens and spilled beyond them. Lucifer shuddered at the impact and felt a thrill beyond description. He took one last admiring glance at himself before he was totally swept into the song of the lights. He sang from the utmost depths of his being.[4]

Near the heavens, something was becoming a place. Lucifer saw a world. It was formless, and covered with waters. The Lord hovered above the depths, and yet was beyond as well.[5] Though he strained his senses, Lucifer could not comprehend the Lord fully.

"Let there be light!" God said. And there was. It burned in a place separate from the dark. And in the same way, land emerged from the roiling waters. Myriads of angels were still singing when planets and suns appeared in the heavens. Lucifer sang with the rest of the stars as things began to live on the land. Creatures filled the waters of the World and crawled upon its land. Other creatures soared in its skies.

Lucifer was puzzled by the different substance or essence of these new creatures. They did not burn like the stars, as he did. Their form had weight and substance alien to his composition. They were curious beings, seemed to be nearly mindless, yet he was intrigued with them, as were the other stones of fire[6] who sang as the new creatures took shape.

And the Son of the Dawn and his countless brothers sang through the universe, helpless to do otherwise, delirious with wonder.

The world was living, covered with vegetation and swarming with creatures, great and small. Other planets revolved in stony silence as the Lord approached the world. The dust of the earth swirled in response, and the

---

4   Job 38:7
5   Genesis 1:2
6   Ezekiel 28:14

Lord shaped it, formed it. The singing of the angels reached new, impossible heights as the Lord breathed into the dust.

The dust became a living being, similar to the other creatures, but bearing some faint reminder of God Himself, it was confined to the surface of the World. The Lord called him, "Man." The Lord spoke with the Man, who was considerably more intelligent than the other creatures. Curiously, Lucifer felt threatened by this newly created thing, even though he sensed his knowledge and power dwarfed that of this Man. Lucifer watched as the Man gave names to the creatures and it stirred resentment within him. Man held dominion over the other creatures of substance. Lucifer sensed that. He wanted this power, this influence for himself.[7]

After a time, the Man slept, and the Lord reached inside the Man and brought forth an essence that was formed into another being. The Man had been shaped from the dust; the Woman shaped from the Man, both by God Himself. The Lord brought her to the Man. The Man recognized the new creature had been formed from his own flesh and bones. He named her, "Woman."[8]

Lucifer felt drawn to her beauty and wanted to possess it. He resented that he had not been the one to name her. He wished to touch her hair as the Man did.[9]

The Lord spoke with the Man and the Woman and gave them authority over the world. The heavens and the earth were now complete. The Lord blessed the seventh day, making it holy, and He set it aside for rest.[10] The universe fell silent.

---

7   Isaiah 14:14
8   Genesis 2:23
9   1 Corinthians 11:5-15
10   Genesis 2:1-3

While all were at rest, Lucifer watched the world and burned silently. Lucifer, the Son of the Dawn, saw the world, that it was good. He wanted to possess it.

⸻ ✻ ⸻

About the story:

In the beginning, God spoke, and "myriads and myriads" (countless numbers) of angels came into being; the Old Testament frequently refers to angels as *stars*. Augustine wrote that, when angels came into existence, they possessed great intellect and knowledge from the very first moment they became aware. Scripture seems to support his conclusion.

The book of Genesis provides the narrative of the creation of heaven and earth, but it does not describe the creation of the angels. However, in the more ancient book of *Job*, God asks Job some very difficult questions. Among them:

> *"Where were you when I laid the earth's foundation? Tell me, if you understand.*
>
> *Who marked off its dimensions? Surely you know! Who stretched a measuring line across it? On what were its footings set, or who laid its cornerstone— while the morning stars sang together and all the sons of God (angels)shouted for joy"*
>
> —Job 38:4-7

So we know the angels were created prior to the creation of the earth, as they were witnesses who sang of the glory of the first moments. We also know that the angels were spoken into existence, just as the heavens and the earth were, because Psalm 148 says so.

Praise the LORD *from the heavens; praise him in the heights above.*
Praise him, all his angels; praise him, all his heavenly hosts.
Praise him, sun and moon; praise him, all you shining stars.
Praise him, you highest heavens and you waters above the skies.
Let them praise the name of the LORD, *for at his command they were created,*
and he established them for ever and ever—he issued a decree that will
never pass away.

—Psalm 148:1-5

Only God is omnipresent, only He exists everywhere at once. Angels are finite beings. They must be *somewhere.* Therefore, in all likelihood, God created the heavens first, and then the angels that would dwell in them.

Angels (as well as the sun, moon, stars, planets, plants, and animals) were spoken into existence by the Lord. Man, however, was crafted out of the earth and God personally breathed the breath of life into his nostrils. Woman was crafted from some portion of the man's body, and presented to the Man by the Creator himself. The Creation of Man and Woman, then, was much more personal and intimate than the creation of the angels.

All the angels that will ever be came into being prior to the creation of the earth. Jesus said that angels do not multiply among themselves.[11] God created only a single Man and a single Woman, but they were distinguished from the angels by God's command to be fruitful and to multiply. Humans were created to reproduce among themselves. Angels were not.

The Bible tells us angels are of different ranks, of different levels of power, and are (when glimpsed by human beings) strange to behold. Scripture does not give us all the details we crave on the different types of angels, but does provide scattered bits of information. The *Cherubim* and *Seraphim* are among the most powerful ranks of the angels; the *Watchers* are apparently the foot soldiers of the host of heaven, the lower ranking spiritual forces. Archangels are above

---

11 Matthew 22:30

all; the Bible names *Michael* as one,[12] and *Gabriel*, perhaps, is another. Ancient Jewish writings beyond the Bible indicate there are at least two more and the names *Raphael* and *Uriel* are probably the most prominent names offered by those writings. The concept of four archangels was frequently explored by great artists during the Middle Ages, but the Bible declines to specify an exact number of archangels.

The book of *Tobit* is part of the *Apocrypha*, a set of Old Testament books that are considered somewhat sacred, but secondary, by the Catholic Church. Neither the Protestant church nor the Jews consider these books to be part of the Old Testament canon of sacred books. In *Tobit*, Raphael declares himself to be "one of the seven holy angels who present the prayers of the saints and enter into the presence of the glory of the Holy One."[13] This reflects the author's belief there were seven archangels, and Raphael was among them.

And then, there is Satan, otherwise known as Lucifer. The name Lucifer (son of the dawn) was drawn by the ancient Jews from the book of Isaiah:

> *How you have fallen from heaven, morning star, **son of the dawn**!*
> *You have been cast down to the earth, you who once laid low the nations!*
> *You said in your heart, "I will ascend to the heavens; I will raise my throne above the stars of God; I will sit enthroned on the mount of assembly, on the utmost heights of Mount Zaphon I will ascend above the tops of the clouds; I will make myself like the Most High." But you are brought down to the realm of the dead, to the depths of the pit.*
> —Isaiah 14:12-15

On the surface, this prophecy concerns someone who is identified as the *king of Babylon*, but between the lines, ancient Jews and Christians saw the story of Satan himself; a magnificent, angelic being who was so enamored with himself he sought to usurp the very throne of the Creator God who spoke him

---

12 Jude 1:9
13 Tobit 12:15

into existence. The book of Ezekiel provides another piece of Lucifer's story, lurking beneath the surface of a proclamation against the *king of Tyre*:

> *"You were the seal of perfection, full of wisdom and perfect in beauty. You were in Eden, the garden of God; every precious stone adorned you: carnelian, chrysolite and emerald, topaz, onyx and jasper, lapis lazuli, turquoise and beryl. Your settings and mountings were made of gold; on the day you were created they were prepared.*
>
> *You were anointed as a guardian cherub, for so I ordained you. You were on the holy mount of God; you walked among the fiery stones. You were blameless in your ways from the day you were created till wickedness was found in you.*

—Ezekiel 28:13-15

Perhaps we are surprised to see Lucifer described as a *cherub*, as our culture imagines cherubs to be chubby infants with tiny wings. The Bible, however, describes the Cherubim to be among the most powerful angels in existence. When viewed by men, Cherubim are seen as strange beings whose appearance nearly paralyzes human beings with awe.

Jewish and Christian scholars have always believed Lucifer and Michael to be the greatest angels in power and majesty. The Bible makes clear that Michael remained in faithful service to the Lord, while Lucifer, of course, did not. These two powerful angels became magnificent opponents, the leaders of angelic forces of good and evil who are often in direct conflict with each other.[14]

Lucifer was blameless in his ways from the day he was created until wickedness was found in him. While the book of Genesis does not tell the story of the creation of the angels, it does tell the story of the fall of Man, and that of Lucifer as well.

---

14 Jude 1:9 and Revelation 12:7-9

2

In the Garden

Now the Lord God had planted a garden in the east, in Eden; and there He put the man He had formed. The Lord God made all kinds of trees grow out of the ground—trees that were pleasing to the eye and good for food. In the middle of the garden were the tree of life and the tree of the knowledge of good and evil. A river watering the garden flowed from Eden; from there it was separated into four headwaters.

The Lord God took the man and put him in the Garden of Eden to work it and take care of it. And the Lord God commanded the man, "You are free to eat from any tree in the garden; but you must not eat from the tree of the knowledge of good and evil, for when you eat from it you will certainly die."[15]

Lucifer and the other stars of burning stone watched these events unfold with great interest. Lucifer began to explore and test his boundaries in the air between the heavens and the world, and was *roaming throughout the earth, going back and forth on it.*[16] The Son of the Dawn inspected the

---

15   Genesis 2:8-16
16   Job 1:7 and 2:2

many creatures that walked the face of the earth and dwelled in the garden with the Man and the Woman. He found many of them intriguing.

Lucifer saw great potential and power in the lion. After a time, he found he could dwell within the creature. He could interact with the world more directly this way. He could feel the cool grass beneath his feet, relish the strength and speed of the great cat's flesh. Lucifer prowled the garden in the body of the lion, and looked upon the Woman as if he might consume her, take her for his own.[17]

The Woman would often leave the Man and go for walks in the garden, where she would seek out various animals and spend time with them. Lucifer observed that the woman seemed to find the serpent to be the most intriguing animal in the garden.

Lucifer decided to explore the nature of the serpent and find kinship with it. He merged his intellect with the substance of the serpent and began to interact with the Woman.

Now the serpent was more crafty than any of the wild animals the LORD God had made. He said to the woman, "Did God really say, 'You must not eat from any tree in the garden'?"

The woman said to the serpent, "We may eat fruit from the trees in the garden, but God did say, 'You must not eat fruit from the tree that is in the middle of the garden, and you must not touch it, or you will die.'"

"You will not certainly die," the serpent said to the woman. "For God knows that when you eat from it your eyes will be opened, and you will be like God, knowing good and evil."[18] Lucifer felt a thrill. Evil. There was a name for the lust within him, and the lust was consummated as he

---

17 1 Peter 5:8

18 Genesis 3:1-5

fathered the lie[19], elevated his own will over that of the Lord. The woman bonded with him in the lie, and they savored it together. Within the serpent, Lucifer said to himself, *"I will ascend to the heaven, I will raise my throne above the stars of God, and I will sit on the mount of assembly. I will ascend above the heights of clouds, I will make myself like the Most High."*[20]

When the woman saw that the fruit of the tree was good for food and pleasing to the eye, and also desirable for gaining wisdom, she took some and ate it. She also gave some to her husband, who was with her, and he ate it. Then the eyes of both of them were opened, and they realized they were naked; so they sewed fig leaves together and made coverings for themselves.[21] "They hide," Lucifer smiled to himself, "How futile. How pathetic."

As Lucifer watched these events unfold, he sensed a great disturbance in the heavens around him. There was anxious uncertainty as corruption began working its way through the vast universe. The whole *creation groaned and suffered the pains* of this new, unholy birth. Lucifer flexed his will within the chaos and discovered that some of these disrupted forces were responding to his commands.[22] He knew that the Man no longer had the power to *subdue the earth* as he once had; the animals would not easily submit to his rule.[23] Lucifer prompted the lion to roar menacingly in the distance and the Man recoiled in newfound fear. Lucifer, still within the serpent, coiled and hissed at the Woman. She screamed, and clutched herself to the side of the Man.

---

19 John 8:44
20 Isaiah 14:13-14
21 Genesis 3:6-7
22 Romans 8:19-22
23 Genesis 1:28

Lucifer chuckled to himself within the body of the serpent and savored their discomfort. The son of the dawn knew there had been a transfer of power, and that he, not the Man, was now the true *ruler of this world.*[24]

Then the man and his wife heard the sound of the LORD God as He was walking in the garden in the cool of the day, and they hid from the LORD God among the trees of the garden.

But the LORD God called to the man, "Where are you?"

He answered, "I heard you in the garden, and I was afraid because I was naked; so I hid."

And God said, "Who told you that you were naked? Have you eaten from the tree that I commanded you not to eat from?"

The man said, "The woman you put here with me—she gave me some fruit from the tree, and I ate it."

Then the LORD God said to the woman, "What is this you have done?"

The woman said, "The serpent deceived me, and I ate."[25]

The Lord God knew that one of His Cherubim, the one known as the son of the dawn, had merged his essence with that of the serpent. He knew the desires of Lucifer's heart, his desire to rule and control Creation; to control the world and even to challenge the sovereign reign of the Lord God Himself. He summoned the Cherub and the animal he possessed into His presence with the Man and the Woman.

So the LORD God said to the serpent, "Because you have done this,

---

24 John 12:31
25 Genesis 3:1-13

"Cursed are you above all livestock and all wild animals! You will crawl on your belly and you will eat dust all the days of your life.²⁶ You were internally filled with violence and you sinned. Therefore I have cast you as profane from the mountain of God, and I have destroyed you, O covering cherub, from the midst of the stones of fire. Your heart was lifted up because of your beauty; you corrupted your wisdom by reason of your splendor. I cast you to the ground.²⁷ And I will put enmity between you and the woman, and between your offspring and hers; he will crush your head, and you will strike his heel."²⁸

To the woman He said, "I will make your pains in childbearing very severe; with painful labor you will give birth to children. Your desire will be for your husband, and he will rule over you."

To Adam He said, "Because you listened to your wife and ate fruit from the tree about which I commanded you, 'You must not eat from it,' Cursed is the ground because of you; through painful toil you will eat food from it all the days of your life. It will produce thorns and thistles for you and you will eat the plants of the field. By the sweat of your brow you will eat your food until you return to the ground, since from it you were taken; for dust you are and to dust you will return."²⁹

A cold wind swept through the garden. The waters of the rivers were turbulent, and the animals bounded back and forth in confusion. The Man and Woman watched in horror as the lion pounced upon a helpless lamb, tore its flesh, and began to feast upon it. Blood dripped from its jaws. The Man and the Woman were spellbound; retching with disgust, yet somehow fascinated with the carnage. The lion turned toward them and

---

26 Genesis 3:14
27 Ezekiel 28:16-17
28 Genesis 3:15
29 Genesis 3:16-19

Lucifer roared. They turned and ran as Lucifer roared again to hasten their departure, even as he relished their fear.

Winded and emotionally spent, the Man and the Woman wept as they searched for the Lord but could not find Him. The Lord God looked at them, shivering in the cold, and His heart was filled with compassion. The Lord drove the lion away from its prey and cradled the remains of the lamb that was slain. *The Lord God made garments of skin for Adam and his wife and clothed them.*

And the Lord God said, "The man has now become like one of us, knowing good and evil. He must not be allowed to reach out his hand and take also from the tree of life and eat, and live forever." So the Lord God banished him from the Garden of Eden to work the ground from which he had been taken. After He drove the man out, He placed on the east side of the Garden of Eden cherubim and a flaming sword flashing back and forth to guard the way to the tree of life.[30]

The Cherubim were strange, powerful and awesome to behold. Each of them had four faces; those of a man, an eagle, a bull and a lion. Each had four wings, with human hands under the wings. Their straight legs were without knees, and gleamed like burnished bronze. In their midst, the sword darted back and forth among them; it looked like coals of burning fire, and lightning was flashing from it.[31]

Adam and Eve moved through a forest, away from the Garden they had called home. The sky was growing dark and they heard the animals moving in the trees around them. They began to search the strange new land for water and shelter.

---

30 Genesis 3:21-24
31 Ezekiel 1:5-13

Many people hold the belief that Satan and his angels fell together at the dawn of time. We generally imagine that Satan and some angels that followed him held a military-style rebellion against God, and a great battle ensued between the angelic forces of good and evil sometime between the climax of creation and the temptation in the garden; perhaps even before the earth was created.

This scenario stems far more from great works of fiction from the Middle Ages than it does from the Bible itself. This story of the initial fall of Satan and his angels is told by wonderful works like *Paradise Lost* by Milton, and Dante's *Inferno*. In *Paradise Lost*, after losing this incredible battle in the heavens, Satan declares, "Better to rule in hell than to serve in heaven." In *Inferno*, there is an inscription over the gates of hell that famously reads, "Abandon hope all who enter here." Images from these tremendous works of fiction have strongly influenced our culture's view of Satan and hell ever since.

There is some basis in Scripture for the idea that this cosmic battle occurred at the dawn of time. Revelation 12:7-9 tells the story of war in heaven among the angels. Michael and the good angels win the war, and Satan and his evil angels are thrown out of heaven. However, there is no indication in this Scripture of when this battle occurred, or what prompted it. Some scholars believe this great battle took place at the cross of Christ. Scripture tells us that when Jesus died, he assumed control of all of the spiritual forces and sat at the right hand of God. It may well be that this was the moment when the battle occurred. Others believe the battle is yet to come; that Revelation 12:7-9 is a description of Satan's final defeat upon Christ's return to earth. Still others believe that this battle is a description of a timeless battle that began early that continues today and will persist until the end of time.

Intriguingly, elsewhere in Revelation 12, another story is told of the Fall of the Angels. In verses 3-4, it is Satan's influence (not the might of Michael's angels) that brings one third of the angels down to the earth. Clearly, this is a separate event, and very likely gives the play by play of how demons other than Satan came to initially fall from heaven.

Jude 1:6 firmly supports this scenario: "And angels who did not keep their own domain, but abandoned their proper abode, He (God) has kept in eternal bonds under darkness for the judgment of the great day." When the majority of angels left heaven, they left voluntarily, lured by Satan, who had preceded them in rebellion against God.

This was what the ancient Jewish people believed, and early Christians as well: that Satan fell first, alone, in the Garden of Eden. The rest of the angels, tempted by Satan, fell later. Both Isaiah 14 and Ezekiel 28, the two chapters that explain why Satan fell, indicate that he fell alone. Neither passage mentions a battle or other angels falling with him.

Consider also that God's sentence upon Satan in the form of a serpent really makes no logical sense if Satan had already rebelled. The punishment God declares in Genesis 3 would be meaningless of Satan had already fallen from heaven prior to the events in the Garden. Consider also that the sentence indicates that Satan, as a result of his actions, will now be *alone*, separated from all the others of his kind. The sentence of Genesis 3 dovetails quite nicely with the description of Satan's Fall as described in Ezekiel and Isaiah.

Sin and death entered the world upon the Fall of Man, and the whole universe was impacted by these events. It was one man's sin that brought sin and death to the world.[32] All of Creation, the entire universe, was disrupted, by the events in the Garden, and Creation has groaned for redemption and restoration ever since.[33]

If there had previously been a cosmic battle which resulted in the Fall of one-third of the angels, wouldn't the universe already have been impacted with

---

32 Romans 5:12
33 Romans 8:19-22

negative results? As we shall see, angels, both good and evil, serve as God's "operating system" for governing His universe. It does not follow logic, or the progressive revelation of Scripture, to say that Satan and his angels had fallen prior to the Fall of Man. When Man fell, Satan was cast down, and the Creation was no longer whole. The cosmos were dramatically changed as result of a single event where both Man and powerful angel fell simultaneously.

The angel had successfully usurped Man's dominion over the earth. Lucifer became the prince of the power of the air, and sin, death and disease became the hallmark of the fallen earth's reality. As for the Man and the Woman... they were taken from the dust, they would toil in it to get their food, and they would return to it.

At this point, Lucifer began *roaming throughout the earth, going back and forth on it.*[34] He prowled the earth like a roaring lion, seeking someone to devour.[35] It would not take him long to find more victims. And in time, other angels would join him in his quest to corrupt mankind.

---

34 Job 1:7 and 2:2
35 1 Peter 5:8

3

East of Eden

OUTSIDE THE GARDEN, life was more difficult. The Man and the Woman mourned the life in the Garden they had lost, and worked hard to survive in a harsh world. *The Man had relations with his wife and she conceived.*[36] The angels, especially Lucifer, watched with great interest as the new life grew within the Woman. *Now the Man named his wife Eve because she would become the mother of all the living.*[37] And Lucifer *stood before the woman who was about to give birth so that when she gave birth he might devour her child.*[38] The Lord had said that the seed of the Woman would crush his head.[39] God's proclamation gave hope to Eve of a return to the Garden. To Lucifer, it made his hold upon the earth uncertain. The child was a threat that had to be destroyed. Lucifer was enraged with the Woman, and would make war with all of her children.[40]

The birth of the child was painful, as God had foretold. The angels were fascinated with the process. They were unable to marry among themselves

---

36   Genesis 4:1
37   Genesis 3:20
38   Revelation 12:4
39   Genesis 3:15
40   Revelation 12:17

as Adam and Eve did. They could not reproduce.[41] There were myriads of angels, almost beyond number. But all the angels that would ever be already were. And so the Man and the Woman, despite their fallen state, had a relationship that the angels could not duplicate, and a legacy of children which angels could not legitimately share. Though far superior in power and knowledge, some of the angels envied the humans for their unique privilege to be fruitful and multiply.

The first son of Adam and Eve was named Cain, and Eve said, *"I have gotten a man child with the help of the Lord[42]*. Perhaps he is our Way back to the garden."* Adam and Eve lived for many centuries and had many more children.[43]

The angels watched with great interest as a large family grew into a small society. Lucifer, most of all, was fascinated with observing the growing population. While he could not read their minds, he was an earnest student of their behavior. He gained great understanding of how men and women thought. Over time, he found he could silently speak to them, fanning the flames of jealousies and other weaknesses in their character. He enjoyed mingling among the men and women and sowing seeds of discord. It amused him to turn them against each other. Cain, the eldest child, was full of a sense of self-importance because of his mother's high expectations for him. Cain became Lucifer's favorite plaything. Outside the Garden of Eden, men and women could still strongly sense the presence of the Lord, but communicating with Him was now much more difficult than it had been. Cain reviled things he did not understand, and became like an unreasoning animal.[44] Cain committed many evil deeds,

---

41 Matthew 22:30
42 Genesis 4:1
43 Genesis 5:3-5
44 Jude 10-11

and hated his brother, Abel, because he was a good man who honored God.[45]

Abel was a shepherd, and Cain was a farmer who tilled the ground. *So it came about in the course of time that Cain brought an offering to the* LORD *of the fruit of the ground.* Cain was going through the motions, and grudgingly offered the portions of his harvest that were of the poorest quality. *Abel, on his part also brought of the firstlings of his flock and of their fat portions. And the* LORD *had regard for Abel and for his offering; but for Cain and for his offering He had no regard.*[46]

So Cain became very angry and his countenance fell. Then the LORD *said to Cain, "Why are you angry? And why has your countenance fallen?* [7] *If you do well, will not your countenance be lifted up? And if you do not do well, sin is crouching at the door; and its desire is for you, but you must master it."*[47] Indeed, Lucifer had practically taken up residence with Cain, and frequently observed the man from the corners of his hut. He was intrigued with just how far he might be able to lead Cain away from God. Potential saviors that would liberate mankind were to be eliminated quickly. In this way, Satan would keep his rule over the world secure.

Lucifer spoke to Cain in quiet whisperings, and suggested that murdering Abel would solve his problems. Cain's anger and disappointment were just cause for this course of action, Lucifer assured him.[48] After pondering these thoughts for some time, Cain spoke with his brother, and invited him out into the field under the pretense of seeking his advice. *And it came about when they were in the field, that Cain rose up against Abel his brother and killed him.*

---

45 1 John 3:11-12
46 Genesis 4:3-5 and Hebrews 11:4
47 Genesis 4:5-7
48 John 8:44

Then the LORD said to Cain, "Where is Abel your brother?"

Cain replied, "I do not know. Am I my brother's keeper?"

God said, "What have you done? The voice of your brother's blood is crying to Me from the ground. Now you are cursed from the ground, which has opened its mouth to receive your brother's blood from your hand. When you cultivate the ground, it will no longer yield its strength to you; you will be a vagrant and a wanderer on the earth."

Cain said to the LORD, "My punishment is too great to bear! Behold, You have driven me this day from the face of the ground; and from Your face I will be hidden, and I will be a vagrant and a wanderer on the earth, and whoever finds me will kill me."

So the LORD said to him, "Therefore whoever kills Cain, vengeance will be taken on him sevenfold." And the LORD put a mark upon Cain, so that no one finding him would slay him. Then Cain went out from the presence of the LORD, and settled in the land of Nod, east of Eden.[49]

Adam and Eve had been blessed with another godly son, who they named Seth, and he walked in the ways of the Lord as Abel had. Eve felt Seth was a gift from God to replace the son that Cain had murdered. Seth and his descendants walked with the Lord and called upon His name.[50] One of Seth's descendants, Enoch, walked so closely with God that, after centuries of life, he was taken up into heaven without having to experience the pain of death.[51] Enoch, son of Seth knew God as well or better than any man. This could not be said for another man named Enoch, who was the son of Cain. His deeds were evil, even as his father's were.

---

49   Genesis 4:8-16
50   Genesis 4:25-26
51   Genesis 5:22-24 and Hebrews 11:5

The descendants of Cain built a city and named it after Enoch, son of Cain. Lucifer enjoyed influencing the people of the city and encouraged them in new ways to explore the dark side of their nature. The sons of Cain became especially skilled at forming things from bronze and iron, and making music with the lyre and the pipe. Some lived as nomads, and they moved from place to place and lived in tents. Through the centuries, Lucifer cultivated the anger of the sons of Cain. Like their ancestor, the sons and daughters of Cain were a vengeful people.[52]

Methusaleh was the son of the godly Enoch and a descendant of Seth. He lived 969 years and was the father of Lamech, who was the father of Noah. Noah had three sons, and was a man who walked with God in times that were increasingly evil.

Throughout these early times, Lucifer explored creative, new ways to do evil. He found that he had the ability to take upon himself a body of flesh and blood. He had the ability to become physical, and take on the appearance and function of a man. He mated with human women and had children with them. His children became the mighty men of old, men of renown.[53] The ancient Greeks, among others, considered these powerful new men to be gods, or sons of the gods. Many other angels were fascinated with Lucifer's activities, and they saw that the daughters of men were beautiful, and they took wives for themselves.[54]

In time, Lucifer's corruption of the human race lured one-third of the angels to abandon their abode in heaven and come down to the earth and live among human beings.[55] Their mighty offspring were called *Nephilim*; they were the product of unholy marriages between angels and

---

52 Genesis 4:17-24
53 Genesis 6:4
54 Genesis 6:1-2
55 Revelation 12:4, 2 Peter 2:-2-5ff and Jude 6

women.[56] For the fallen angels, these unions were a quest for sexuality and descendants they were not designed to have; for men and women, these marriages offered the prospect of power and immortality for their children. Lucifer had drawn many followers to follow in his footsteps, to go beyond the plans and design of God in a quest to become gods themselves.

Up until this time, men and women had lived many centuries before succumbing to death. When God saw this terrible sin among men and angels, He decided to limit the lifespan of humans to approximately 120 years.[57] *Then the Lord saw that the wickedness of man was great upon the earth, and that every intent of the thoughts of his heart was only evil continually, and He was grieved in His heart.*[58] His creation had been thoroughly corrupted through the unnatural mating between women and angels, and evil had consumed nearly all of mankind as a result. The earth was corrupt in the sight of God and filled with violence.[59]

However, Noah found favor in the eyes of the Lord. Noah was a righteous man, blameless in his time; he walked with God.[60] So God said to Noah, "I must bring an end to all flesh, save for you and your family and two of every kind of animal. Build an ark, and stock it with the supplies to sustain all of these. *For you alone I have seen to be righteous before me in this generation.*"[61]

Then Noah gathered his family and the animals into the Ark, and the Lord closed the door behind him. The flood came upon the earth for forty days, and the waters rose above the mountains. *All flesh that moved*

---

56 Genesis 6:4
57 Genesis 6:3:13-7:1
58 Genesis 6:5
59 Genesis 6:11-12
60 Genesis 6:8-9
61 Genesis 6

upon the earth perished; birds and cattle and beasts and every swarming thing and all mankind. All in whose nostrils was the breath of the spirit of life...died.[62] Noah and his family were the only human beings left alive.

God did not spare the angels when they sinned, but cast them into hell and committed them to pits of darkness reserved for judgment. God did not spare the ancient world, but preserved Noah when he brought a flood upon the world of the ungodly.[63] *And the angels who did not keep their own domain, but abandoned their proper abode, God has kept in eternal bonds under darkness for the judgment of the great day, just as Sodom and Gomorrah and the cities around them, since they in the same way as these indulged in gross immorality and went after strange flesh.*[64]

When the flood waters receded, the residents of the Ark exited it, and Noah built an altar to the Lord and made sacrifices upon it. And the Lord blessed Noah and his sons and said to them, *"Be fruitful and multiply, and fill the earth...*I establish my covenant with you and your descendants." And so the original design of the earth was restored. The fallen angels had been physically removed from the earth, and their unholy offspring had all perished in the Flood, along with the human population they had so thoroughly corrupted. And God blessed Noah and his family with the same words He had used when He had blessed Adam and Eve, in a Garden where everything they saw was good.[65]

"Be fruitful and multiply," the Lord said to Noah and his family.

---

62 Genesis 7:1-22
63 2 Peter 2:4-5
64 Jude 6-7
65 Genesis 9:1ff

After reading this story, you may feel you took a wrong turn at the Bible and ended up in the middle of Greek mythology. But think about it... what if Greek mythology had some basis in fact?

I think most people, when reading the story of Noah and the Flood, ask themselves the question, "WHY?" Why would God wipe out most of the population of the earth? What was the situation in the time of Noah that was SO EVIL that God would take such a drastic action? People back then were sinful, but people are just as sinful today....or are they? What sin would have prompted God to destroy every living thing on the face of the earth? The Bible responds to the question, but with our modern mindsets, we desperately grope for alternative answers.

The ancient Jewish people and the earliest Christians all believed that angels fell from heaven because of their sexual sin in the time of Noah. It was not until centuries after Jesus ascended to heaven that this explanation of things began to be questioned. As Western thought and science became more and more based on Greek philosophy, the more repugnant the idea that angels and humans had once mated became. After that, a parade of alternative explanations became popular, none of which can be supported by Scripture. All of the alternatives twist Scripture like a pretzel in order to avoid the truth. It is a truth that makes us squirm, to say the least.

God destroyed every living being on the earth because His creation was seriously messed up. Men and angels had crossed the border between species. Who is to say that the animal kingdom had not been similarly corrupted? Apparently, the evil that caused God to destroy the earth with a Flood was perverse and pervasive. It seems that nearly every living thing was thoroughly compromised by evil.

Let's assume that we have correctly identified the sin that caused God to destroy the world with a Flood. Perhaps the next question that arises might be HOW could angels mate with human women? Angels are spiritual beings. How could they be physical enough to mate with women?

Rather than pause now to fully explain the answer, let it simply be said that the Bible says that angels have the power to take on the form of physical, functional human beings. When God allows it, angels can manifest bodies that walk, talk and touch like human beings. Bodies that eat food like human beings and seem to be human in every way.

In the coming pages, our exploration of the story of the angels will reveal just how possible the impossible story of Genesis 6 really is.

4

Towers and Powers

Praise the Lord! Praise the Lord from the heavens! Praise Him in
the heights! Praise Him, all His angels! Praise Him, all His hosts!
Praise Him, sun and moon! Praise Him, all stars of light! Praise
Him, highest heavens, and the waters that are above the heavens.
Let them praise the name of the Lord, for He commanded and
they were created. He has also established them forever and ever,
He has made a decree that will not pass away.

Psalm 148:1-6

HIS NAME IS Michael, a name that means, "who is like God?" He is an
archangel, one of the chief princes in heaven.[66] He walks upon the
holy mountain of God, in the midst of the stones of fire with the other
princes.[67] He and his brother, Gabriel, are two of the few beings able to
stand in the presence of the Lord.[68] Long ago, one of their number had
been filled with violence, fallen from the midst of the stones of fire, corrupted by reason of his splendor. He had been cast to the earth.[69] Lucifer

66   Jude 9 and Daniel 10:13
67   Ezekiel 28:14
68   Luke 1:19
69   Ezekiel 18:16-17

no longer dwelled in the highest heaven. The heavens mourned, and the Creation groaned.

At the dawn of time, God had created the angels; myriads of them, beyond number. As God spoke the universe into existence, God placed the angels in charge of various aspects of creation. God remained in control of the galaxies, but chose to administer the elements, the planets and the weather by establishing the spiritual powers He created as stewards of various aspects of His new reality. When Man and Lucifer fell in the Garden of Eden, the universe was seriously disrupted by the birth of evil. The universe was no longer pristine; sin, death, destruction and decay polluted what had been perfect in the beginning. The universe itself groaned for restoration.[70]

By deceiving Adam and Eve, Lucifer had seized their rightful role as rulers of the earth. He became prince of the power of the air, and he ruled the dimension between heaven and earth.[71] Michael and the other chief princes wondered at how Lucifer's treachery had resulted in his accumulation of dark power and authority. A new and terrible aspect of reality was now in Creation, and the angels pondered the mystery; why did the Lord allow such a thing to take place?[72]

Lucifer, forever banished from the highest heavens and the company of the other angels, amused himself by sowing discord and destruction among men and women. Taking physical bodies of various sorts, controlling the elements of weather, and invisibly influencing the behavior of men were among the great powers he possessed during this time.

Eventually, one third of the angels in heaven were enthralled by Lucifer and his activities. They decided to follow Lucifer, to leave heaven and descend to the earth. For a time, they enjoyed the freedom to assume

---

70 1 Corinthians ?
71 John ?
72 1 Peter 1:12

human bodies and to mate with human women. During this period, evil reached levels beyond description upon the earth. The angels and their children enjoyed great influence and power until the Lord declared an end to things. Then there was war in heaven. The angels' administration of the elements of weather was thrown into chaos by the conflict. The Flood that God had decreed was the result, and it destroyed all Nephilim (angel/human children) and most men and women.

The war raged in heaven; Michael and his angels were waging war with the dragon, with Lucifer, and his angels. At the end of the battle, there was no longer a place for them in heaven, and Lucifer was thrown down, and his angels with him.[73] God committed these angels to pits of darkness, where they would await the judgment of the final Day.[74] Then Michael laid hold of the dragon and threw him into the abyss, and shut it and sealed it over him so that his power to deceive nations was diminished for many years, until he would be released near the end of time for a brief period.[75]

The Pit was, and is, not a physical location, but rather a dimension which restricts the activity of the fallen angels, also known as demons, upon the earth. Though they no longer have the ability to assume the form of humans or animals, they still influence the world of men. The physical elements of the universe (such as weather) are still governed by the angels, both good and evil, who were constantly in a state of conflict. Demons also hold the power to dwell within humans, a condition that is called "possession".[76] God had declared that this would be the state of existence for angels for centuries, until the Pit is opened during the Tribulation, the final days before Christ's return.

---

73 Revelation 12:7-9
74 2 Peter 2:4-5
75 Revelation 20:1-3
76 Luke 8:22-39

While the fallen angels no longer enjoy the freedom to influence the world to the extent they once had, they remain united under Lucifer to sow discord among the men and women who dwell upon it.[77] Throughout history, demons have lured men and women into worshipping them instead of the one true God.[78]

After the Flood and his imprisonment in the dimension known as the Pit, Lucifer continued to control many aspects of the world, but could not exceed the boundaries that the Lord established. Lucifer ruled the world, limited by the Pit, but God remained supreme over Lucifer. This fact was never doubted by any of the fallen angels.[79]

Now all the angels observed the activities of men and women with great interest; they longed to understand men and women, and the plan God had for human history.[80] In the beginning, Lucifer had fallen because he had believed he could become like God. He drew Adam and Eve into the same sin in the Garden. He drew most of mankind and one-third of the angels into the same snare when he lured angels to mate with women. All of these tragic situations had a common theme; Satan knew the pride of men and angels could be exploited so that those who fell into temptation served the purposes of Lucifer instead of God.

Now after the days of Noah, men and women multiplied. They all spoke one language, and became unified in purpose to build a great city, with a tower that would reach the heavens. Once more, Lucifer had drawn these hapless humans into believing they could make a name for themselves, to be equal to God, and reach into the heavens.[81] Lucifer knew they could not gain physical access to the heavens by building a tower. Men,

---

77 James 3:14-16
78 Psalm 106:34-38 and Ezekiel 16:20-21
79 James 2:19
80 1 Peter 1:12
81 Genesis 11:1-4

however, did not, and Lucifer enjoyed stoking their brazen attitudes as they proudly engaged in their futile efforts to equal God.

This arrogant project did not, of course, escape the notice of the Lord. *So the L\ORD scattered them abroad from there over the face of the whole earth; and they stopped building the city. Therefore its name was called Babel, because there the L\ORD confused the language of the whole earth; and from there the L\ORD scattered them abroad over the face of the whole earth.*[82]

Some time later, *there was a man in the land of Uz whose name was Job; and that man was blameless, upright, fearing God and turning away from evil.*[83] *Now there was a day when the sons of God* (both good and evil angels) *came to present themselves before the L\ORD, and Satan also came among them. The L\ORD said to Satan, "From where do you come?"*

Then Satan answered the L\ORD and said, "From roaming about on the earth and walking around on it."[84]

The Lord and Satan had a discussion about Job. Satan believed that Job was loyal to God simply because he had great wealth and a good family. God decided to allow Satan the opportunity to test his theory. *Then the L\ORD said to Satan, "Behold, all that he has is in your power, only do not harm the man himself." So Satan departed from the presence of the L\ORD.*[85]

In the days that followed, Satan worked among the people known as the Sabeans. He incited them to raid Job's lands. The Sabeans, under the influence of Satan, killed Job's servants and stole his oxen and donkeys.

---

82 Genesis 11:8-9
83 Job 1:1
84 Job 1:6-7
85 Job 1:8-12

Lucifer worked in similar fashion among the Chaldeans, who slew more of Job's servants and stole his camels. Then Satan exerted his influence over the elements of the weather to destroy Job's flocks and shepherds with lightning. He also caused a great wind to collapse the house of Job's oldest son, killing all of Job's children.[86]

Despite all of the evil things that Satan caused to happen, Job continued to have faith in God. He fell to the ground in worship and cried out, *"Naked I came from my mother's womb, and naked I shall return there. The LORD gave and the LORD has taken away. Blessed be the name of the LORD."*[87]

When Satan again appeared before the Lord, he argued that if Job were in fear of his life, if he were afflicted with disease, then he would curse God. The Lord again allowed Satan to test his theory. Satan left the presence of the Lord and caused Job to be afflicted with disease; his body was covered with boils and sores. Job's wife encouraged him to curse God and die. However, Job remained faithful to the Lord, insisting that those who trust in God must be prepared to accept difficult things in life as well as blessings.[88] Job had faith that God would eventually redeem him from his painful circumstances; if not in this world, then in the world God would rule after the resurrection of the dead.[89]

Some people believe that God created the earth, and then left the planet and its people totally on their own, to make their own decisions, and to live or die as a result. While this is not a correct view of how God maintains His Creation, there is a certain amount of truth to it. All angels and human beings

---

86 Job 1:13-19
87 Job 1:20-22
88 Job 2:1-9
89 Job 19:25

possess free will. On a daily basis, they make choices that honor God or result in evil. However, ultimately, all of history remains in the hand of God; no event can happen unless He allows it to happen. Also, God does not leave us totally on our own; the Bible clearly teaches that, from time to time, God invades the reality of men and women and takes direct action. We call these invasions "miracles". The greatest miracle of all is when God became Son of Man in Bethlehem.

In the beginning, when Man, Woman and Satan fell, death and disease entered the world, and from that moment on were largely under Satan's control. Satan exerted a certain amount of control over the elements of the weather; this influence greatly increased, we presume, when one-third of the angels in heaven joined him in his fallen state.

The passages of Scripture referred to above clearly demonstrate that a vast portion of our reality is under the control of Satan and his fallen angels. Satan has the ability to influence people to commit war and crimes upon each other; to lead them into prideful rebellion against God; to afflict them with disease, even kill them; and to control the elements of the weather to bring disaster upon those he wishes to afflict.

As such, the activities of Satan and his demons have a tremendous impact on the existence of human beings and our daily lives. As Jesus Himself observed, Satan is the ruler of this world (John 12:31). Satan cannot be all places at all times, but is the ruler of all demons (Matthew 9:34) and therefore has the ability to influence events all over the world.

However, Satan and his demons do not possess the power to override the will of God anymore than we do. God elects to allow fallen angels and human beings to make choices which often result in death and destruction. However, God, through the Holy Spirit, restrains us from totally destroying ourselves. God also directly intervenes and frequently rescues people from the destruction that angels and humans bring about.

People who are skeptical of God's existence or kindness frequently make observations like, "If God is so good, why are people starving in Africa?" The answer is that, for the most part, God has left the process of earthly government to whims of men, under the influence of angels, both good and evil. While God may directly intervene from time to time, He has left large portions of the destinies of His creatures in the hands of the creatures themselves. However, everything that men and angels say and do is in line with God's will. His design of thinking beings caused history to follow His perfect plan. Free will and God's sovereign rule of the earth seem to be contradictions, and to our human minds they are. Yet, Scripture teaches both aspects of this paradox and we must accept that these seemingly contradictory forces co-exist in God's universe.

People also ask, "Why did God destroy all those people with that tsunami?" The answer is that destructive weather is the result of the activities of evil spiritual powers. Such destruction may well be instigated by evil angelic forces. Their ability to do so is clearly demonstrated by the story of Job as recorded above.

So, are we totally at the mercies of demonic forces? No. God has always reigned supreme over all spiritual powers. Jesus demonstrated His own mastery over those powers when He was on earth. In Luke 8:22-25, Jesus and His disciples are in a boat, threatened to be overwhelmed by a storm. Jesus commands the demonic forces in charge of the storm to cease the activity. Later in Luke 8, Jesus casts a legion of demons out of a possessed man. These demons were "imploring Him not to command them to go away into the abyss." (8:31) This passage shows that Jesus' authority was clearly recognized by the demons themselves. Further, the Bible teaches that, when Jesus ascended into heaven, all spiritual powers in the universe were made subject to Him.

When we consider these things, the importance of prayer quickly becomes more evident. When we pray for someone's healing, we pray for wisdom for physicians and their treatments. Whether we recognize it or not, we are also praying that the dark spiritual forces which may be causing the disease will be repelled.

When we pray for God's protection for loved ones when they travel, we are praying that dark angelic forces that may seek to harm them are restricted from doing so. When we pray for world peace, we are praying that the dark spiritual influences that incite men to war and destruction might be overcome by spiritual forces of light. Our struggle in this world, Paul tells us, is not against flesh and blood, not against people, but against the rulers, the powers, world forces of darkness, and spiritual forces of wickedness in the heavenly places.[90]

Why do these ideas seem so primitive, so mythological? Quite frankly, it is because for decades, if not centuries, our churches and schools have not taught us much about the spiritual reality around us. Our culture violently rejects the idea of Satan and demons. Most people consider angels to be decorations at Christmas time, and little more. During 2014, there was a huge uproar in the press because Pope Francis declared his belief that Satan is a real being. Imagine that! The leader of the largest Christian denomination in the world comes under fire because he believes that angels and demons are part of our reality.

It has been said that one of Satan's greatest weapons is that people refuse to believe that he exists. The Bible says that Satan is constantly prowling like a roaring lion, looking for someone to devour.[91] It is much easier for Satan to destroy people who don't even believe he exists, who don't know how to fight him, who never see him coming.

Scripture says when we resist Satan, firm in our faith, God will strengthen us in the effort.[92] Paul tells us that we need to employ special spiritual weapons in this conflict.[93] If we resist the devil, James says he will flee from us.[94]

---

90 Ephesians 6:12
91 1 Peter 5:8
92 1 Peter 5:9-10
93 Ephesians 6
94 James 4:7

In Acts 26, Paul tells King Agrippa the story of how Jesus knocked him off his horse and gave him a new mission in life. Jesus told Paul his new purpose was to open the eyes of the Jews and Gentiles "so that they may turn from darkness to light and from the dominion of Satan to God." (verse 18) This mission, one every Christian shares with Paul, is not symbolic or figurative. It is a factor of major importance in the fabric of our earthly reality. It is of even more importance in determining the nature of our eternity.

The majority of the world unknowingly serves a powerful, invisible, spiritual force who rules the world through a network of other fallen angels. These beings are capable of wielding disease, elements of weather, other human beings, and even death against their enemies. Their objective is to bring death and destruction and damnation to as many human beings as possible. They bear special hatred against human beings who have allied themselves with the Creator God upon whom they turned their backs.[95]

The Bible teaches that Satan and his demons are real, and are dedicated to our destruction. Because the spiritual forces of evil are limited by the invisible chains of the Pit, their ability to influence the earth, while great, is less than it was before the times of Noah. However, in the end times, they will be released from the Pit, and will regain their former abilities to bring even more incredible evil into the world of men. The book of Revelation gives an incredible preview of what that world will be like.

As we continue to examine the story of the angels, we will learn more about the means that dark spiritual powers have employed to disrupt and destroy the world of men and women. As a result, we have the opportunity to be better equipped to grapple with the dark realities that we prefer to ignore.

---

95   Revelation 12:17

5

Angels Walk Among Us

Now Abram lived in the land of Ur, and the Lord called him out of that country in order to journey to a land He had promised to give him and his seed. So Abram, his wife Sarai, and his nephew Lot left the city of Haran and set out for Canaan. The Lord would later seal the promise of descendants by making a covenant with Abram; this was a promise that could not be broken.[96] God would change the names of the couple to Abraham and Sarah to confirm their role in His plan.

Some years later, God Himself appeared in the form of a human being to Abraham when he was camped by the oaks of Mamre. The Lord brought two angels with Him; these angels had also taken the form of human beings. The Lord and the two angels were fully functional in the human sense. Abraham served them food, and they ate it; he also washed their feet. The Lord, in the form of a human being, had a dialogue with Abraham about the promised birth of his son, Isaac; a conversation which Sarah overheard and later joined.[97] God told Abraham of His plan to judge, and probably destroy the corrupt cities of Sodom and Gomorrah. Abraham begged the Lord not to destroy the cities if ten righteous men could be

---

96 Genesis chapters 12-15
97 Genesis 18:1-15

found within them, and the Lord agreed. After that, the presence of the Lord departed, and the two angels who remained proceeded to journey on to the city of Sodom.[98]

As the two angels, apparently beautiful in their physical appearance, passed through the city of Sodom, they attracted the attention of the city's residents. After the angels reached the home of Lot, *the men of Sodom, both young and old, surrounded the house and said to Lot, "Where are the men who came to you tonight? Bring them out to us so that we may have intercourse with them!"*[99] Lot's refusal to surrender the angels angered the crowd and the wicked men threatened to do even worse to Lot before they had their way with his guests. The angels opened the door of Lot's home, reached out and grabbed Lot, bringing him back into the safety of the house. Then the angels struck the men in the crowd blind, so they were unable to find Lot's door.[100]

The two angels told Lot they were going to destroy the place, and advised him to gather his family and lead them out of town. Lot persuaded his wife and daughters to leave, but his sons-in-law thought he was joking. When Lot hesitated to leave, the two angels *seized his hand and the hand of his wife and his two daughters* and brought them outside the city.[101]

The angels commanded Lot and his family to flee to the nearby town of Zoar and not to look back. The Lord, through the two angels, rained fire and brimstone out of heaven and the towns of Sodom and Gomorrah were consumed. Lot's wife looked back at the destruction, disobeying the angels' command, and was transformed by them into a pillar of salt. The

---

98   Genesis 18:17-19:1
99   Genesis 19:5
100   Genesis 19:6-11
101   Genesis 19:12-16

next morning, Abraham rose and gazed down at the pillars of smoke that were rising from the ruins of Sodom and Gomorrah.[102]

Some time after this, Abraham and his wife were blessed with a son, who they named Isaac, just as the Lord had told them. Years later, God put Abraham to the test by instructing him to take his young son up on a mountain and to offer him as a sacrifice. However, as Abraham raised the knife to kill his son, the angel of the Lord called out to him and stopped the sacrifice. Abraham then sacrificed a ram which was trapped in a nearby thicket instead of his son. After the sacrifice, the Lord repeated His promise to Abraham to give him many descendants. *"In your seed all the nations of the earth shall be blessed, because you obeyed My voice,"* the Lord told Abraham.[103]

Many years later, Jacob (the son of Isaac and grandson of Abraham) was fleeing the wrath of his brother, Esau, whom he had deceived. He spent the night at a place called Luz, and slept on the ground with a stone as his pillow. As he slept, he dreamed of angels that were ascending and descending a ladder that stretched from the earth into the heavens. The Lord Himself stood above the ladder, and the angels, and made the same promises to Jacob that He had made to Abraham. Jacob said, *"How awesome is this place! This is none other than the house of God and the gate of heaven!"* Jacob renamed the place "Bethel".[104]

Years later, as Jacob was going back to his homeland, he remained in great fear that his brother, Esau, would kill him upon his return. However, God had commanded Jacob return home, and he was committed to doing so. Jacob sent gifts to Esau, hoping to appease him, but a messenger told him that Esau was on the way to meet him with 400 men at his side. Now

---

102   Genesis 19:17-29
103   Genesis 22:1-18
104   Genesis 28:10-19

greatly afraid, Jacob sent his wives and children across the river Jabbok, but he remained alone on the other side of the river during the night.

All through the night, Jacob wrestled with a man. When the man merely touched his thigh, Jacob's hip was dislocated. Jacob came to understand that this man was actually the angel of the Lord Himself. God had taken human form in order to confront Jacob on that fateful night.[105] Perhaps the encounter prevented Jacob from abandoning his family to save himself; perhaps this was the way the Lord gave him the courage and strength to meet his brother face-to-face.

⤜∞⤛

There are many appearances of angels in the Bible. Contrary to popular belief, angels never appear as women. When they appear as men, they do not have a single set of wings, as depicted in many works of art and in our manger scenes. There are a number of instances where angels are described as having wings; usually each angel is described as having four or six wings, not two. And the bodies attached to those wings are incredibly strange in appearance, with multiple faces (some being animal faces) and sometimes even covered in eye balls! In most cases, when angels are at their most spectacular, it is when they are viewed in heaven and/or the presence of God's throne.

When angels make an earthly visit to God's people in the Bible, they almost always appear as men. Sometimes, they are extraordinary in appearance, with limbs of bronze or other spectacular features. More often, however, they seem to be nearly indistinguishable from ordinary men. They do the things that men do; they walk, talk, sit, and eat. They touch people and people can touch them.

---

105   Genesis 32:3-32

In ancient Jewish culture, they believed that the act of *eating* served as proof that someone was human and not a ghost. This is clearly illustrated by one of Jesus' appearances before the disciples shortly after His resurrection:

> *Jesus stood in their midst and said to them, "Peace be to you." But they were startled and frightened and thought that they were seeing a spirit. And He said to them, "Why are you troubled, and why do doubts rise in your hearts? See My hands and feet, that it is I Myself; touch Me and see, for a spirit does not have flesh and bones as you see that I have." And then He showed them His hands and feet. While they still could not believe it because of their joy and amazement, He said to them, "Have you anything here to eat?" They gave Him a piece of a broiled fish, and He took it and ate it before them."*
> —Luke 24:36-43

Jesus' appearance before the apostles was not enough to convince them He was not a ghost. Even His offer to let them touch Him and examine His wounds left them in doubt. However, when He ate the piece of fish, they were finally convinced that He was an actual human being. In similar fashion, when the Angel of the Lord and two other angels sat and ate with Abraham, they established that they were present with him in functional human bodies; bodies that were probably somewhat similar in nature to Jesus' resurrection body.

When the two angels proceeded to the city of Sodom, the debauched men of the city found them extremely attractive and all of them wanted to have sex with them. They certainly believed it was possible for them to do so; they were prepared to break down the door of Lot's home to get at them.

As the two angels gathered Lot's family to bring them out of the city before it was destroyed, they again displayed that they were physical beings. The angels not only touched Lot, his wife and his daughters; they practically dragged them out of the city.

After we consider these matters, where angels are clearly able to manifest themselves as functional humans, then the idea of angels falling from heaven in order to mate with human women no longer seems outlandish, but entirely possible.

Some claim to have Scriptural proof that such marriages could not possibly have occurred. Most frequently they appeal to a passage where Jesus declares that angels do not marry. "For in the resurrection they (men and women) do not marry nor are given in marriage, but are like angels in heaven." (Matthew 22:30) This statement says nothing about angelic abilities to take human form, or whether they ever mated with women. Jesus is comparing the resurrection bodies of those who believe in Him to the conditions angels enjoy *in heaven*. We know that angels do not reproduce among themselves in heaven. The passage says nothing about what occurred on earth during the time of Noah, not even indirectly.

We know that God, of course, can do anything. If He can speak a universe into existence, He could certainly manifest Himself as a man. The fact that He has, of course, is the very backbone of our Christian faith. As for the angels, by all appearances, the Bible teaches they can become fully functional flesh and blood when permitted to do so by God. This leads to many wonderful and disturbing possibilities within the world of men, doesn't it?

6

The Word

*I*N THE BEGINNING *was the Word, and the Word was with God, and the Word was God. All things came into being through Him.*[106] *He is the image of the invisible God, the firstborn of all Creation.* All angelic forces were created by Him and for Him: all thrones, dominions, rulers and authorities in the heavens.[107] There is nothing in existence that is not subject to the Word, though this reality is not yet visible to mankind.[108] When the Word became man, He was known as Jesus.

Some say it was the Word who walked with Adam and Eve in the Garden.[109] That the Word, accompanied by two angels, spoke with Abraham on the plains of Mamre. The Word Himself declared that He was the ladder that Jacob saw in his dream, the stairway to heaven upon which angels ascended and descended between earth and heaven.[110] Later, it was said that the Word wrestled with Jacob, and blessed the man, and named him

---

106 John 1:1-3
107 Colossians 1:16
108 Hebrews 2:8
109 Genesis 3:8
110 John 1:51

Israel.[111] The Word appeared in the burning bush and spoke to Moses about the deliverance of the sons of Israel from captivity in Egypt.[112]

They say the Word stood in the path of Balaam and his donkey with a sword in His hand.[113] Decades later, sword once again in hand, the Word declared to Joshua that He was the captain of the Lord's heavenly host, the angelic forces that fought for Israel.[114]

The Word would again appear as a man before Gideon, and commission him to deliver God's people from the hand of Midian. When Gideon placed an offering before Him, he touched the meat and bread with the tip of the staff in His hand, and fire sprang from the rock beneath it as the Word vanished before Gideon's eyes.[115] Not long after, the Word appeared to the parents of Samson to announce the great warrior's upcoming birth. Manoah (the father of Samson) asked the Word for His name, even as Jacob had done, centuries before. The Word replied that His name was wonderful, beyond comprehension. As Manoah and his wife made an offering to the Lord, the Word ascended toward heaven in its flames.[116]

Centuries later, the Word appeared as a "son of man" and guided three young Jewish men out of Nebuchanezzar's fiery furnace.[117]

The Word was God, and with God. At key points in the history of the salvation God had for men and women, the Word would visit them, within

---

111 Genesis 32:24ff
112 Acts 7:35
113 Numbers 22:22ff
114 Joshua 5:13-15
115 Judges 6:11ff
116 Judges 13:11ff
117 Daniel 3

a temporary veil of flesh, so He could be with them in a way they could understand. So He could speak with them as one would with a friend.

Then, in the fullness of time, God sent the Word to be actually born of a woman, a virgin, in order to make the redemption of men and women a reality.[118] When the Word became flesh, God revealed His plan for history and His kind intentions for men and women. What had been a mystery to both men and angels was now revealed; God intended to make men and women His sons and daughters. He would reconcile all things in heaven and earth to Himself through the giving of His Son, Jesus Christ.[119] The angels, since the dawn of time, had longed to understand this mystery.[120] And now the incredible wisdom of God was revealed as the salvation story was being unfolded before them.[121] Perhaps now the angels could know why some of their own had been allowed to abandon their place in heaven, and why men and women had also fallen, and evil had been allowed to distort all of creation.

So Gabriel, one of the chief princes of the angelic forces loyal to the Creator, was sent to a young maiden in Nazareth, to offer her the opportunity to be the vessel in which the Word would become man.[122] This would be no short visit for a special occasion. This time, the Word would actually become flesh and dwell among men and women.[123]

"Your son will be great and will be called the Son of the Most High," Gabriel told young Mary. "The Holy Spirit will come upon you, and the power of the Most High will overshadow you. Though a virgin, you will conceive, because nothing is impossible with God." After young Mary

---

118 Galatians 4:4
119 Ephesians 1:3-12
120 1 Peter 1:12
121 Ephesians 3:8-11
122 Luke 1
123 John 1

agreed to serve God in this way, Gabriel left her. And the Word became the blessed fruit of her womb. [124]

When the days were completed for her to give birth, Mary and her husband, Joseph, had sojourned to Bethlehem. The village was crowded, and they took shelter in a manger, where the Word was born.

An angel of the Lord appeared to some shepherds in a nearby field and said to the frightened men, "Do not be afraid; for behold, I bring you tidings of great joy which will be for all the people. Today in the city of David there has been born for you a Savior, who is Christ the Lord."

Suddenly, a multitude of angels appeared with that angel and the skies nearly burst with their praise for God, the Word, and the plan for man's salvation.[125]

Satan, though somewhat restricted by the Pit, remained the prince of the power of the air and the ruler of the present age. When the Son of God was born in Bethlehem, Satan attempted to kill the young Word with the armies of Herod.

Another angel was sent by God to warn Joseph, the husband of Mary, and their family left the region until the danger had passed. [126] Angels made sure that the Word would not be silenced before He was heard.

Years later, the Word, now known as the man Jesus of Nazareth, was led by the Holy Spirit into the wilderness in order to fast and pray, and be tempted by Satan. Satan showed Jesus all the kingdoms of the world in a moment in time, and said to Him, "I will give you this domain and its

---

124 Luke 1-2
125 Luke 2
126 Matthew 2 and Revelation 12:4

glory, for it has been handed over to me, and I give it to whomever I wish. Therefore, if You worship before me, it will all be Yours."

Jesus did not dispute that Satan held the power to make and keep such a promise. The Word answered Satan, quoting from the Law of Moses, "It is written, 'you shall worship the Lord your God and serve Him only.'"[127]

Satan knew that Jesus could summon angels, and tempted Him to use this power to glorify Himself and prove His identity to the people of Israel. He led Jesus to Jerusalem and had Him stand on the pinnacle of the Temple. Satan then invited Jesus to throw Himself off the temple and be rescued by the angels He commanded. When Jesus, again quoting the Law of Moses, refused to do so, Satan left Jesus until a more opportune time.[128] After the devil departed, angels came to Jesus and saw to His needs.[129]

The struggle between Jesus and Satan's kingdom continued throughout the earthly life of the Son of God; as the Word expelled demons and cured disease, He was showing His Kingdom to be superior to that of Lucifer's. Perhaps it was the night Jesus was betrayed that Satan considered the "more opportune time" to tempt Jesus to depart from the will of God the Father. It was there that Jesus expressed in prayer His hope that the cup of God's wrath might not be poured out upon Him. His struggle was so great that His sweat was like drops of blood. However, in the end, Jesus accepted the Father's will, and an angel from heaven appeared to Him, giving Him added strength.[130] Later, Judas, who was possessed by Satan,[131] appeared with soldiers in the hour of darkness, Jesus commanded His disciples not to resist the soldiers. After all, Jesus told them,

---

127   Luke 4:1-8
128   Luke 4:9-13
129   Matthew 4:11
130   Luke 22:41-44
131   John 13:27

He could have summoned legions of angels to His side had He desired to do so.[132]

During that night, Satan afflicted the disciples as well. He influenced the very heart of Judas Iscariot, causing him to betray Jesus to the chief priest.[133] Centuries before Christ, Satan had received permission to devastate the life of Job, a good man who sought to follow God faithfully. In this same fashion, on the night Jesus was betrayed, Satan was given leave to attack Simon Peter. Jesus warned Peter that Satan had been granted permission to "sift (him) like wheat."[134]

The next day, Satan thought he had achieved his greatest victory when the Son of God died upon the cross. However, Satan discovered that his authority had been snatched from him, and it was his power that was nailed to the cross. Satan and his dark angelic powers were disarmed and humiliated by the cross of Christ.[135]

When the Word had died in order to bring men and women to God, He was dead in His flesh, but alive in His spirit. The spirit of the Word went to the Pit, and made proclamation to the fallen angels who had been imprisoned there since the time of Noah. In the Pit, the Word declared His victory over all spiritual forces of wickedness. By the time He ascended into heaven to the right hand of God the Father, all angels and spiritual powers and authorities were now subject to the His authority.[136]

Three days after the Word died on the cross, an angel descended from heaven, causing an earthquake, and the angel rolled away the stone that sealed His grave. Soldiers guarding the tomb quivered in fear at the sight

---

132 Matthew 26:52-53
133 John 13:2
134 Luke 22:31
135 Colossians 2:14-15
136 1 Peter 3:18-22

of the angel, whose face was like lightning. The angel spoke to the women who had come to anoint the dead body of the Word, and told them He had risen from the dead.[137]

Forty days later, the risen Word stood with His disciples on the Mount of Olives and bid them farewell for a time. As He ascended into heaven, two angels appeared beside the disciples and told them that the Word would return from heaven, descending to earth in the same way they had seen Him leave it.[138]

After His death, the Word had descended to the lowest parts of the earth in death, even to the Pit. But when He arose from the dead and ascended into heaven, He led all spiritual forces as captives in His parade of victory.[139] The Word had disarmed the rulers and authorities, and made a public display of them declaring His triumph over every angelic force in Creation.[140]

When the Word had walked the earth as a man, Lucifer once offered Him the kingdoms of the world. Now, the Word sits at the right hand of the Father, and all Creation is held together and overseen by Him. At the mention of His name, even the knee of Lucifer must bow. Even Lucifer must confess the Word is Lord.[141]

The Word has physically left the world of men, at least for a while. Lucifer and his angels are allowed to continue to roam and exercise limited rule over the earth for a time. But the Word will come again, to judge the living and the dead. And when He comes, the very stars will fall from the skies and all the angelic powers in the heavens will be shaken and

---

137 Matthew 28:1-6
138 Acts 1:9-11
139 Ephesians 4:7-10
140 Colossians 2:15 Hebrews 1:3-4 and Ephesians 1:19-21
141 Philippians 2:9-11

overthrown. The sign of the Son of God will appear in the sky, and the angels of the Word will gather the children of God from the face of the earth, and the Word will be with them forever.[142] The men and women who recognized the authority of the Word in this life will serve as judges of the fallen angels in the next.[143] Satan and the other angels who opposed the Word will be thrown into the eternal fire that has been prepared for them.[144]

<hr />

The story of Jesus did not begin in Bethlehem, of course. In fact, the story of Jesus truly has no beginning, because He is and always was God. This dynamic fact often becomes lost in the shuffle when people debate who Jesus is/was. Jesus was not a man who became God. He was God made man.

The Bible tells the story of a number of angelic appearances that involve a very special entity known as the *Angel of the Lord*. This is no ordinary angel, but a special representation of the Lord Himself. Some say it is simply an angel with a special mission from God. A number of important Jewish rabbis believed that the Angel of the Lord was either Gabriel or Michael.[145] Other scholars say that these appearances are *theophanies*: a personal appearance by God the Father Himself at critical points in Biblical history. Still others label them *christophanies*; appearances by the Second Person of the Trinity in temporary human form prior to His incarnation as one of us at Bethlehem. Distinguished theologian Millard Erickson concludes, "While none of these interpretations is fully satisfactory ...either the second or the third seems more adequate than the first."[146]

<hr />

142 Matthew 24:29-31
143 1 Corinthians 6:3
144 Matthew 25:41
145 Ronald H. Isaacs, <u>Ascending Jacob's Ladder: Jewish Views of Angels, Demons, and Evil Spirits</u>, Northvale, NJ, Jason Aronson, Inc., 1998, p.14
146 Millard Erickson, <u>Christian Theology</u>, Grand Rapids, MI, Baker Books, 1998, p.468

For many reasons, the majority of Christian scholars who are well-informed on the subject lean toward the idea that Jesus Christ was the being known as the Angel of the Lord who appeared upon occasion in Old Testament history. At the turn of the twentieth century, a man named Geerhardus Vos taught theology at prestigious Princeton University for 39 years. According to Reformed theologian John Murray, Vos was the best ever at finding the true meaning of Scripture. That's no small compliment.

Vos presented a very convincing case that the Angel of the Lord is the Second Person of the Trinity, the Son of God who would later become Jesus. Thus, the Angel of the Lord would refer to God (the Father) in the third person, just as Jesus did. He would, at the same time, be an "uncreated being" who fully represents God the Father. Also, the only essential difference between the "body" of the Angel of the Lord and that of Jesus is that one is temporary, before Bethlehem, and the other is eternal, after the Son was incarnated in the womb of Mary of Nazareth.[147] Other noted theological figures such as John Calvin and many of the early leaders of the church also believed that the Angel of the Lord described in the Old Testament was Jesus Christ.[148]

While Jesus Christ quite likely took human-like form as the being known as the Angel of the Lord, it is important to remember that *He is infinitely different from any angel.* Colossians 1:16 states clearly that all things, visible and invisible, were created *by* and *for* Jesus. He is *Creator*, not *created*. A number of religions, both ancient and more recent, have inaccurately portrayed Jesus as being a mere angel, the most powerful and glorious created being. Some religions indicate that Jesus was/is Michael the archangel, and some that Jesus is the angelic "brother" of Satan. The Bible does not support these views.

147 Geerhardus Vos, Biblical Theology of the Old and New Testaments, Grand Rapids, MI, William B. Eerdman's Publishing Co., 1948, pp.72-78
148 John Calvin, Institutes of the Christian Religion, Grand Rapids, MI, William B. Eerdman's Publishing Company, reprinted 1995, p. 145

According to Philippians 2, Jesus existed in the form of God and then "emptied Himself" and took the form of a man. He died in this humble state, and then was exalted over every being in existence; "those who are in heaven, on earth, and under the earth." When Jesus became a man, he shared our status as beings that are currently lesser than angels. But when He sat down at the right hand of the Father, He became greater than any angel could ever be.[149]

The early Christians who followed Jesus did not have the privilege of easy access to Scriptures as we do. In order to remember important Biblical truth, they would memorize simple creeds. These creeds contained essential portions of the story of salvation in very simple form. Among the most enduring of these is the Apostles' Creed.

> *I believe in God, the Father Almighty, the Creator of heaven and earth, and in Jesus Christ, His only Son, our Lord: Who was conceived of the Holy Spirit, born of the Virgin Mary, suffered under Pontius Pilate, was crucified, died, and was buried. He descended into hell. The third day He arose again from the dead. He ascended into heaven and sits at the right hand of God the Father Almighty, whence He shall come to judge the living and the dead. I believe in the Holy Spirit, the holy catholic church, the communion of saints, the forgiveness of sins, the resurrection of the body, and life everlasting. Amen.*

The Apostles' Creed did not exist in this form during the time Jesus' disciples were alive. Though they undoubtedly composed and taught creeds in various forms, the Apostles' Creed as we know it probably was not in this form until at least 300 years after Christ ascended into heaven. Pieces of the Apostles' Creed, however, can be traced back to the first and second century.

For the last few hundred years at least, there has been a great deal of debate over the portion of the Apostles' Creed that says that Jesus *descended into hell.*

---

149 Hebrews 1:3-6

1 Peter 3 indicates that after His death, Jesus went to some location in the afterlife, but there are a variety of explanations with respect to exactly where he went and what he did there.

This was not true of the early church. Both the ancient Jews and early Christians believed that the fallen angels had been confined to the Pit in the time of Noah. These Christians also believed that Jesus, between His death and resurrection, went to the Pit to declare His victory over the dark spiritual forces that opposed Him. This event was so significant in the beliefs of early Christians that it was frequently included in the short list of the most important things to remember about their faith. Many early creeds contained this information in some form.

When we read the Bible, we see it as the story of God, intertwined with the story of men and women. Rightfully so, because it is. However, what many theologians have ignored and even denied for many years is that the story of the angels is told by the Bible as well. The history of angelic beings is intertwined with the story of God, just as surely as is the story of mankind.

When people who study the Bible recognize that fact, then a number of controversies, including Jesus' descent to hell, are easily unraveled. Many so-called "problem passages" in the Bible are no longer a problem once we decide to accept the truth of the story the Bible clearly tells.

7

Gods and Monsters

THE ANCIENT BOOK of *1 Enoch* says that, during the time of Noah, angels left their abode in heaven in order to take wives for themselves. These same angels taught men to make swords, knives, shields, breastplates, mirrors, bracelets and ornaments. They also taught the use of paint, makeup dyes, and precious stones, sorcery, divination, astronomy and astrology. The world was forever altered by these things.[150] Men and women considered these angels and their offspring to be as gods. When God destroyed the earth with the great Flood, these angels were confined to the Pit, where their activities would be restricted until the Final Judgment.[151] Their mighty children, the Nephilim[152], perished along with mankind in the Flood.

Centuries after Noah, Jacob and his twelve sons settled in Egypt because of a world-wide famine. In the decades that followed, they multiplied into a nation within Egypt; the Egyptians eventually felt threatened and enslaved them. Like Canaan, the land of Egypt was corrupted by practices that God detested; they sought out ghosts and mediums and sacrificed

---

150 1 Enoch 8
151 2 Peter 2:4-5
152 Genesis 6

to idols and demons.[153] The people of Egypt, like those of Canaan, dedicated their lives to the demons they worshipped and were condemned by the prophets of God.[154] Perhaps the severe judgment that the Lord brought upon the people of Egypt were the natural consequences of their demonic worship and dedication to the dark arts.

Before Moses led the people of Israel out of captivity in Egypt, the Lord sent plagues upon the Egyptians in order to exact judgment upon them and upon the "gods" they served.[155] Ironically, the Lord utilized the demons themselves to carry out the judgment.[156] The Psalmist writes that the Lord used "a deputation of angels of evil" to strike the Egyptians with the various plagues.[157] In this way, God displayed His superiority over all the other "gods", the spiritual forces in heaven; angels, both good and evil. God demonstrated clearly that He governs the whole earth through His dominion over the angels.[158] The demons that fashioned themselves as Egyptian gods were proven powerless to resist God's will.

After the exodus from Egypt, Moses led Israel into the dessert and met with God on Mt. Sinai, where he received the Ten Commandments, also known as the Law of God. The Law of God itself was ordained through angels;[159] thousands of them were present on Mt. Sinai when the Law was given to Moses.[160] Ironically, the commandments delivered by angels declared that no angel, fallen or not, was to be an object of worship by the people of God.[161] When God, Moses and the angels met on Mt. Sinai,

---

153 Isaiah 19:3 and Leviticus 18:3
154 1 Corinthians 10:20
155 Exodus 12:12
156 1 Samuel 4:7-8
157 Psalm 78:49
158 Psalm 89:5-8, Zechariah 1:9-11 and 6:4-5
159 Galatians 3:19
160 Psalm68:17
161 Exodus 20:1-4

there was fire and darkness, gloom and whirlwind, and the sounds of trumpets and thundering voices so unearthly that the people of Israel begged to hear them no more. Even Moses, the great man of God, trembled in fear.[162]

After forty years in the desert, the people of Israel were finally ready to enter the Promised Land. God appointed Joshua as the new leader of Israel, as Moses would not be permitted to enter Canaan. Moses had issued a number of warnings to the people of Israel prior to his death, especially about worshipping idols. He told the people that worshiping gods other than Yahweh was actually the worship of demons and that such actions would estrange them from the one, true God.[163]

Moses also warned the people of God of the dangers of practicing dark arts that trafficked with demons. He told Israel not to adopt the ways of Canaan, which included human sacrifice of their own children, divination, witchcraft, interpreting omens, sorcery, casting spells, telling the future or calling up the spirits of the dead. Moses also cautioned the Israelites that the Lord actually detests those who practice such things.[164] People who indulged in these dark arts were apparently at great risk of being possessed by the very demons they sought to harness or control.[165]

After giving the people his blessing, Moses ascended Mt. Nebo, where God showed him the Promised Land. Then Moses died, and God Himself buried him somewhere in the land of Moab.[166] According to the ancient book, *The Assumption of Moses*, there was a battle between Satan and Michael the Archangel for Moses' body. Centuries later, a man named

---

162 Hebrews 12:18-21

163 Deuteronomy 32:15-19

164 Deuteronomy 18:9-14

165 Acts 16:16-18

166 Deuteronomy 34

Jude referred to this struggle in a brief letter that Christians would come to consider sacred Scripture.[167]

The twelve spies that Moses had sent into the Promised Land said that *Nephilim*, the mighty giants that were the result of angel/human marriages, were living in Canaan.[168] The intermarriage of angels and humans had been the reason that God had destroyed all life on earth with the Flood. During the centuries between Noah and Moses, a number of other angels had descended to earth and taken wives to themselves, though not as many as during the time before the Flood. These giants were constantly at war with the people of God.[169]

When Joshua led the people of Israel into the Promised Land, the land of Canaan, God sent an angel before them to assist Israel in driving out or destroying the people of Canaan. God instructed Israel to do this so that they would not worship their gods or follow their terrible practices.[170] Perhaps the resumption of angel/human marriage in Canaan was the reason that God commanded the Israelites to totally eliminate certain segments of its population.

In the times of Noah, the Lord demonstrated that this violation of His created order would be met with the obliteration of the humans and hybrid human/angels, as well as the imprisonment of the offending angels themselves within the Pit. Even the majority of animals were subject to this harsh punishment. The sentence God passed upon the Amalekites in the time of Saul was eerily similar; Israel's first king was commanded to destroy every man, woman, child and animal among them.[171] Perhaps

---

167 Jude 1:9
168 Numbers 13:25-33, Genesis 6:4
169 1 Chronicles 20
170 Exodus 23:20ff
171 1 Samuel 15:1-3

the crimes of the Amalekites bore similarity to the sins of the people in Noah's time as well.

Saul did not obey the command of the Lord to destroy the Amalekites completely. Centuries later, his failure would nearly result in the genocide of every person of Jewish origin. Haman, a descendant of Agag, king of the Amalekites, nearly succeeded in totally obliterating the people of God.[172] The seed of Satan, whether they be literal or spiritual children of demons, do not hesitate when given the opportunity to totally eliminate their enemies.

Like Saul, the people of Israel also disregarded God's instructions, and did not completely expel the Canaanites from the Promised Land. They lived with them, and married among them, and over time began to practice their abominations.[173] As God had warned, the Israelites fell into worshipping the idols of Canaan, dedicated to angels who had fallen from heaven. The Israelites, following the ways of Canaan, participated in human sacrifice to these false gods; they sacrificed their own children to demons.[174] Some of the kings of David's line were faithful to the Lord; others fully participated in the worship of other gods.

David was Israel's greatest king and a man after God's own heart. Unlike Saul, David was devoted to carrying out the Lord's wishes, and he eventually succeeded in expelling nearly all of God's enemies from the Promised Land.[175] He spent his days in a lifelong struggle against both the sons of men and the sons of angels.

When he was little more than a boy, David had witnessed a huge man who cursed the Lord violently and mocked the armies of Israel. The giant was

---

172 Esther 3
173 Ezra 9
174 Psalm 106:34-38 and Ezekiel 16:20-21
175 Acts 13:22

known as Goliath of Gath, for he lived in that Philistine city.[176] However, Goliath was not a Philistine by birth; he was descendant of Anak. The sons of Anak were identified by Moses as being Nephilim, the hybrid children of angels and women who grew to be the mightiest of warriors.[177] When the young man who was the ancestor of the Messiah went to battle the great giant with only a sling, he was not facing a mere man. The chosen one of God was facing the actual son of a demon. Among the endless battles between the seed of the woman and the seed of the serpent, this encounter has proved to be among the most memorable in history. Through David, the Lord demonstrated that His chosen people did not need to possess physical superiority to obtain victory over the sons of darkness. Thousands of years ago, the daughters of Israel sang of David's great victory.[178] This song has echoed through the centuries ever since.

Some of the remaining sons of dark angels dedicated themselves to the destruction of Israel, especially their anointed leader. Much later in life, King David grew weary in battle and was nearly killed by a giant named *Ishbi-benob,* who was from the line of Anak, just as Goliath was. These sons of Anak were just some of the Nephilim who lived in Canaan.[179] After this close call, David's men would no longer allow him to join them in battle, because they feared Israel might lose their great leader.[180]

After King David died in his bed of old age, the people of Israel continually turned back toward worshiping idols. When Rehoboam, son of Solomon and grandson of David, became king, ten tribes broke away and formed the northern nation of Israel. Rehoboam continued to reign over the kingdom of Judah and the remaining two tribes. The southern nation of Judah, ruled by David's heirs, frequently turned away from

176 1 Samuel 17
177 Numbers 13:33, Genesis 6:4
178 1 Samuel 18:6-7
179 Numbers 13:33
180 2 Samuel 21

God but would repent upon occasion. The northern kingdom of Israel, on the other hand, quickly turned away from God, and none of their kings were dedicated to the Lord.

Elijah was the greatest prophet during the time of the kings, and at one point he believed himself to be the only true believer in the northern kingdom. He challenged 450 prophets of the false god Baal to a contest on top of Mt. Carmel. The prophets of Baal danced around an altar, begging their demon god to send fire to consume their sacrifice. In order to gain Baal's favor they danced around the altar and cut themselves until their blood gushed all over their bodies. The God of Israel suppressed any response from dark angelic forces in answer to the pleas of these false prophets. However, when Elijah called upon the Lord, God sent fire from heaven to consume his sacrifice, even though it had been repeatedly drenched with water.[181]

King Manasseh of Judah was the son of Hezekiah and a descendant of David. Hezekiah had been a godly king, but upon his death, Manasseh built high places of demon worship, placed idols in the Temple, practiced witchcraft and divination, dealt with mediums and spiritists, and even sacrificed his own son to demons. His dark leadership led the entire nation to become even more evil than Canaan itself.[182] Prophets of God continually warned the nation of Judah that God would not tolerate this disloyalty much longer. The people didn't listen, and Israel was taken into captivity by the armies of Babylon and Jerusalem and the Temple were destroyed.

Nebuchadnezzar, the king of Babylon, was obsessed with the worship of false gods and demanded that all of his subjects join him in doing so, including his captives from Israel. A young Israelite named Daniel interpreted some of Nebuchadnezzar's dreams, and upon more than one

---

181   1 Kings 18
182   2 Kings 21:1-9

occasion, the king spoke of the superiority of the God of Israel. However, Nebuchadnezzar continued to pursue false gods and was driven insane for a time as a result. His eventual recognition of the one, true God rescued him from his madness.[183]

Throughout the days that the people of Judah were exiled in Babylon, angels continued to watch over them, even while they were in foreign lands. The three young Hebrew men known as Shadrach, Meshach and Abednego were protected from the flames of a furnace by an angel.[184] Daniel should have been devoured by lions, but an angel shut the mouths of the fearsome beasts.[185]

After a time, it appeared that the mating of angels with human women came to a halt, although the possibility that an angel loyal to God could fall into temptation with a woman apparently continued into New Testament times.[186] By the time of Jesus, the fallen angels, now known as demons, were generally confined to the dimension known as the Pit. This restricted, but did not eliminate, the ability of the demons to exert influence on men and women and their world. Apparently, they were able to escape, at least partially, the chains that the Pit had upon them.[187]

While fallen angels could no longer take the physical form of men, they could possess human beings and afflict them in other ways. The gospels record several stories of demon possession that clearly reflect the desire of the demons was to destroy the very humans in which they dwelled. One demonic spirit that Jesus encountered attempted to drown his host, threw him into fire, gave him convulsions, and made him deaf and mute.[188]

183 Daniel 1-4
184 Daniel 3
185 Daniel 6:22
186 1 Corinthians 11:5-10
187 Luke 8:31
188 Mark 9:14ff

Luke tells how a large group of demons caused a man to wander naked through tombs of the dead for years.[189]

Paul the Apostle makes it clear that fallen angels remain a threat to mankind, even after the death and resurrection of Jesus Christ. To this day, these gods and monsters disguise themselves as angels of light and still seek to enslave human beings and to lead them to destruction.[190]

⸺⸺

The ancient book of 1 Enoch was composed by fervent Jews about two hundred years before the birth of Jesus Christ. The first portion of this work, called *The Book of the Watchers*, contains an elaborate and fantastical version of how the angels fell into sin with human women. The book was considered sacred by first century Jews and Christians, and much of the imagery about heaven and hell that inspired artists and writers in the Middle Ages came from the pages of 1 Enoch as well. The Bible does not confirm all the details of this religious book, but there are echoes of 1 Enoch throughout the New Testament, and it is quoted in the book of Jude.[191] The part of the story that tells of angels being imprisoned in the Pit during the days of Noah is confirmed in several places; most notably in Jude, 1 Peter, and 2 Peter.[192]

Both inside and outside of the Pit, fallen angels became the false idols and gods worshipped by the ancients. Merriam-Webster offers two definitions for "God"; one is capitalized, the other not.

---

189   Luke 8:27ff
190   2 Corinthians 11:13-15 and 2 Timothy 2:26
191   Jude 14
192   1 Peter 3:18-22, 2 Peter 2:4-10, Jude 6-7

God: the supreme or ultimate reality: as **a:** the Being perfect in power, wisdom, and goodness who is worshipped as creator and ruler of the universe

god: a being or object believed to have more than natural attributes and powers and to require human worship; *specifically* **:** one controlling a particular aspect or part of reality

As we have seen, the Bible says that angelic forces of light and darkness have the ability to influence many aspects of our reality, including the behavior of individuals, the activities of governments and tribes, and the elements of weather. Essentially, angels are gods of a sort, though they are not the ultimate authority in any aspect of existence; whatever they do is either permitted by God or initiated by Him. While fallen angels are beings of great power, they will be held responsible for the tragedies they initiate. In Psalm 82, God acknowledges that angels are gods (to some degree) and will be held responsible for showing partiality to the wicked and neglecting the poor and oppressed. The psalm also indicates that God is ultimately in charge of the reality in which these false "gods" are allowed to operate. Psalm 97 calls upon all the hosts of heaven to worship God, as He is above all gods, real or imagined.

Knowing this, let's revisit some familiar words from Exodus, as God reveals one of His primary commandments to Israel:

> *Then God spoke all these words, saying, "I am the LORD your God, who brought you out of the land of Egypt, out of the house of slavery. You shall have no other gods before Me. You shall not make for yourself an idol, or any likeness of what is in heaven above or on the earth beneath or in the water under the earth. You shall not worship them or serve them; for I, the LORD your God, am a jealous God, visiting the iniquity of the fathers on the children, on the third and the fourth generations of those who hate Me, but showing lovingkindness to thousands, to those who love Me and keep My commandments.*
>
> Exodus 20:1-6

This commandment is not only a prohibition against idols or manmade gods. It is a command not to worship the angelic beings whom God has allowed to be instrumental in administering the world around us. It is a command not to worship angels, good or evil.

The threat that fallen angels present to God's plan for salvation did not diminish in New Testament times, as Paul observes:

> *But I am afraid that just as Eve was deceived by the serpent's cunning, your minds may somehow be led astray from your sincere and pure devotion to Christ. For if someone comes to you and preaches a Jesus other than the Jesus we preached, or if you receive a different spirit from the one you received, or a different gospel from the one you accepted, you put up with it easily enough.*
>
> 2 Corinthians 11:3 -4

In 2 Corinthians, Paul goes on to observe that Satan disguises himself as an angel of light, and false religious teachers do the same.[193] Jesus says clearly that such false teachers are sons of the devil from a spiritual standpoint. He says that Satan is the father of lies, and that absolutely no truth resides within him. Anyone who waters down or changes the message of God that is given through the Bible and Jesus Christ is, whether they realize it or not, serving the father of lies.[194] This being, this dark angel and his allies, has no mercy upon those who follow him, knowingly or unknowingly.

Are angels still capable of taking human form today? Is sexual interaction with human women still possible? According to what we have learned, such activity is no longer possible for angels who have already fallen, as they are restricted by the dimension/chains called the Pit. The temptation to mate with human women apparently remains an active possibility for angels who

---

193 2 Corinthians 11:13-15
194 John 8:42-45

have remained faithful to the Lord. This is the reason for Paul's admonition to Christian women in 1 Corinthians 11:5-11. He tells the women to practice modesty in order to prevent these unnatural unions from reoccurring. This warning seems unclear and vague to us, but remember that Paul was not writing his letter for you and me (not knowingly, anyhow). His audience would not have needed more information to firmly grasp his meaning. Consider the following quote from another important Jewish religious writing from the first century. The passage is not from Scripture; however, it does provide us with some background on how the Jewish people viewed this issue in the first century.

> *Accordingly, my children, flee from sexual promiscuity and order your wives and daughters not to adorn their heads and their appearances so as to deceive men's sound minds. For every woman who schemes in these ways is destined for eternal punishment. For it was thus that they charmed the Watchers, who were before the Flood. As they continued looking at the women, they were filled with desire for them and perpetrated the act in their minds. Then they were transformed into human males...*
>
> Testament of Reuben 5:4-6

Recall that the Watchers are a rank or class of angels. Within the Bible, this term appears only in the book of Daniel[195]; however, it frequently appears in ancient Jewish writings outside of sacred Scripture, especially in 1 Enoch. From a Scriptural standpoint, it remains possible today for an angel loyal to God to fall from heaven by taking human form and mating with a human woman. Even more disconcerting, the book of Revelation indicates that, in the last days of the earth, demons will be released from the restrictions that prevent them from assuming human form once again.[196] These last days, Jesus says, will be like the days of Noah; the darkest of times.[197] During the final

195 Daniel 4
196 Revelation 9:2
197 Luke 17:26

days of the earth, Satan and his angels will operate with the same kind of freedom that they had during the days that led up to the Flood. Perhaps the ranks of Nephilim at the end of time will include the beast himself, the man of lawlessness who will dominate the kingdoms of the earth during the days of Tribulation.[198] Movies like *The Omen* and *Rosemary's Baby* may touch lightly upon a very uncomfortable truth.

Less fantastic, but of even greater concern, is the fact that the father of lies remains active in our world today in spreading false ideas about God. The Bible indicates there was a steady stream of false teachers throughout Old and New Testament times, and that this will continue right through to the end of the world. Idols and false gods, physical and spiritual, are still being worshipped all around the world. The earth itself has increasingly become an object of worship within the last fifty years. False prophets, like the dark angels that influence them, still look good to us, even on TV; but Scripture warns us that, beneath the sweetness of a message that is easily accepted, lies sinister intent.[199] To accept "truth" that fits our preferences results in our destruction.[200] While we are reluctant to admit this, dark angelic forces know it full-well.[201]

Thankfully, Jesus assures us that His word will never pass away.[202] Despite the best attempts of dark spiritual forces, the Word of God will remain available to those given eyes to see it and ears to hear it.[203]

---

198 Revelation 13 and 11:7
199 Matthew 7:15
200 Matthew 7:21-23
201 James 2:19-20
202 Matthew 24:35
203 Revelation 3:5-6

8

War in Heaven and on Earth

I N THE BEGINNING, there were no fallen angels and no fallen men. When Adam and Eve fell, they were expelled from the Garden of Eden. Two Cherubim, the most powerful class of angels, were posted at the entrance to the Garden to prevent the return of the first humans, and perhaps that of the first fallen angel as well. The Cherubim each wielded a flaming sword; this was the first visible sign of the war that had begun in heaven and on earth. Men began killing men shortly after. Cain had the blood of Abel on his hands, but so did Lucifer, who led Cain to do the deed.

The struggle between good and evil spiritual forces began when Satan tempted Adam and Eve. The fall of Lucifer from heaven had removed all truth from his character; one of the most beautiful and powerful of angels became the father of lies and a murderer at the beginning of time.[204] At first, Satan was the only dark angel contesting with myriads of angels who remained dedicated to the Lord. Centuries later, one third of the angels left their domain in heaven to descend to earth in the days of Noah. They were lured from the heavens by Satan to join his dark activities upon the earth.[205]

---

204 John 8:44
205 Revelation 12:3-4

The war in heaven reached new intensity when Satan and his demons were imprisoned in the Pit. [206] A great angel of light, perhaps Michael the archangel, laid hold of Satan and threw him in the Pit where his power would be somewhat restricted until the last days of the earth.[207] The great angel who threw Satan into the Pit would remain at his post, restraining Satan's power, until the appointed time.[208]

Not long after, on the plains of Shinar, men still spoke a single language and built a tower in an attempt to reach heaven. Then the Lord came down and scattered men to various nations, and further divided them by causing these nations to speak different languages. [209] Angels of light and darkness gravitated toward different regions of the earth; certain angels were given dominion over the various nations.[210] The human governments of each nation became deeply intertwined with the spiritual rulers that exerted invisible influence on the affairs of mankind.[211]

The wars that were constantly taking place on earth were a reflection of the ongoing battle among forces of good and evil in the heavens.

Satan and his dark angels relished the violence of war, and took special pleasure in directing the armies of men toward the destruction of people who followed the one, true God.[212] God Himself had prophesied this when He explained to Adam and Eve the consequences of their actions in the Garden of Eden.[213] Job was a prosperous follower of the one, true God, and Satan himself was anxious to destroy the man. Satan utilized

---

206   Jude 1:6-7
207   Revelation 20:1-3, 2 Peter 2:4ff
208   2 Thessalonians 2:6-10
209   Genesis 11:4-9
210   Daniel 10:13 and 12:1
211   Psalm 82
212   Revelation 12, especially 7-9 and 17
213   Genesis 3:15

lightning, wind and murderous raiders to destroy most of Job's family and property with the natural and supernatural means at his disposal.[214]

Centuries later, when the people of Israel were enslaved by Pharoah, and he refused to release them, God sent a band of destroying angels to force the king of Egypt's hand. Plagues of insects, frogs, disease, hailstones, lightning and death were among the weapons used by these angels to bring the nation to its knees.[215] Shortly after the people of Israel finally were allowed to depart, Pharoah changed his mind and pursued them with his soldiers and chariots. The military might of the nation of Egypt was obliterated by the waters of the Red Sea.[216] In dealing with Egypt, God clearly demonstrated His sovereignty over angels, demons, nations and wars in both heaven and earth.

God directed the people of Israel into the Promised Land, and personally participated in the invasion. God promised to send His angel before them to help them expel or destroy its evil population. The Angel of the Lord appeared to Joshua and declared He was the captain of the Lord's host. The sword in His hand clearly indicated that God and His angels would be heavily involved in the conquest of Canaan. The Lord spoke to Joshua and gave him some very strange instructions on how to destroy the walls of the city of Jericho. The walls of the great city collapsed after the Israelites marched repeatedly around them.[217] Some time later, God even stopped the progress of the sun in the sky to allow Israel the time needed to destroy the forces of the pagan kings of Jerusalem and Hebron.[218] The Angel of the Lord later withdrew His promise to fight for Israel because they failed to tear down the altars of

---

214 Job 1 and 2
215 Psalm 78:43-51
216 Exodus 14
217 Joshua 5:13-6:5
218 Joshua 10

false gods as He had commanded them.[219] Even though God had repeatedly shown Himself the deliverer of Israel, the people could not resist the temptation to worship the very forces that were dedicated to their destruction.

For the next few centuries, the incomplete conquest of Canaan left the people of Israel vulnerable to raids and attacks by various groups of hostile neighboring kingdoms. From time to time, Israel would repent of their idolatry and cry out to the Lord for deliverance from oppression. God would periodically raise up spiritual and military leaders, known as judges, to help His people. The Angel of the Lord Himself appeared to Gideon, to instruct and enable him to lead his people to victory over the Midianites.[220] The Angel returned to announce the birth of Samson, who was given great strength through the power of God's own Spirit to battle against the Philistines.[221] When the king of Canaan threatened Israel with his superior forces and 900 iron chariots, the judges Deborah and Barak were appointed to lead the armies of Israel. They were joined by angels who caused earthquakes, rains and the flood of the river Kishon, resulting in the deadly chariots being mired in mud.[222] As King David would later write, the Angel of the Lord encamps around those who fear Him.[223]

Centuries later, after Israel had divided into two nations, Elisha, the successor to the great prophet Elijah, was threatened by the Arameans, who surrounded his city with a great army and chariots. When Elisha's servant expressed his dismay to the prophet, Elisha replied, "Do not fear, for those who are with us are more than those who are with them." Elisha prayed, and God opened the eyes of his servant, who saw that the mountain near them was filled with horses and chariots of fire; angels sent

---

219 Judges 2:1-5
220 Judges 6:11ff
221 Judges 13:3ff
222 Judges 5; 5:20 (stars) is a reference to angels
223 Paslms 34:7

to protect the prophet of God from physical harm. Elisha prayed and a strange blindness fell upon the Arameans, and he led them into a place where peace was negotiated with Israel.[224]

In the southern kingdom of Judah, during the reign of Hezekiah, (a good king descended from David) the Assyrians threatened Jerusalem with a huge army. The prophet Isaiah declared that, because of the blasphemous arrogance of the Assyrians, God would send them back home humiliated. The Lord sent an angel who destroyed all the Assyrian officers and their best warriors.[225] In all, over 185,000 Assyrian soldiers died in a single night. The Assyrians slunk back home in defeat.[226]

Just over 500 years before the birth of Christ, the Temple in Jerusalem was destroyed by King Nebuchadnezzar's armies, and the people of Judah were carried into exile. Among them was a young man named Daniel, who was deeply dedicated to the God of Israel. During his many years in Babylon, the Lord gave Daniel the ability to know and interpret the dreams of others.

Daniel interpreted King Nebuchadnezzar's dream of a great statue made of gold, silver, bronze and clay. This dream foretold of the coming empires of Persia, Greece, and Rome, and how all kingdoms of the earth would be put to an end by the kingdom of God. Daniel's revelation of the dream and its meaning resulted in his being appointed to a position of great influence in Babylon.[227] When Nebuchadnezzar dreamed a second time, he saw an angel. This angel was from a class of angels known as Watchers, and judgment was pronounced upon the king by decree of

---

224   2 Kings 6:8ff

225   2 Chronicles 32:9ff

226   2 Kings 19:35ff

227   Daniel 2

these Watchers. As a result, Nebuchadnezzar was driven mad for a time, but was restored to his throne when he cried out to the God of heaven.[228]

Over the decades, Daniel served several kings well. One of them, Darius, was maneuvered into throwing Daniel into a den full of lions. However, an angel came to protect Daniel, and prevented the lions from harming him.[229]

Daniel also received fantastic dreams and visions from God. During the first year of King Belshazzar's reign, he had a vision of beasts and kingdoms and of God Himself, as well as the Messiah, whom Daniel called the Son of Man.[230] Belshazzar's reign came to an abrupt end when a disembodied hand appeared in his banquet hall and scrawled a prophecy of doom upon its wall.[231] Years later, while Daniel was in an extended period of fasting and prayer the angel Gabriel appeared to Daniel and shared great words of prophecy with him.[232]

Some time after that, when Daniel was with some companions near the Tigris River, he saw an angel with a fantastic appearance of bronze, fire and lightning, whose voice thundered in his ears. The men with him could not see the angel, but felt a great sense of dread and fled from the scene. Daniel collapsed to his knees and the angel helped him back to his feet and spoke to him.

This angel told Daniel of unseen battles in the heavens between angelic forces of light and darkness. Daniel's prayers had risen to heaven, but a great angelic battle had to be fought before the angel could come to Daniel's side. The angelic messenger of the Lord identified Michael,

228   Daniel 4
229   Daniel 6:22
230   Daniel 7
231   Daniel 5
232   Daniel 9:20ff

the chief angelic protector of Israel, as his greatest ally, and his greatest opponent was the dark angelic prince of Persia. After restoring Daniel's strength, the angel said he was going to return to the battle with this angelic prince of Persia and the spiritual forces aligned with Greece. The angel told Daniel that only he and Michael were standing firmly against these dark angels. As Daniel listened, the angel shared great prophecies about the Messiah, the fates of the nations of the earth, and events at the end of the world. Joined suddenly by two additional angels, Daniel's visitor hovered over the river and gave Daniel parting words that included a promise of his resurrection at the end of the world.[233]

Daniel wrote down the words given him by the angel, which provide a rare look at the unseen world around us. They tell of war between fallen angels, who seek to destroy mankind, and angels loyal to the Lord, who do God's will in protecting men and women from the dark spiritual forces. The invisible wars that take place in heaven are echoed by the wars among men that we see.

Zechariah lived during the same period as Daniel, and was one of the last of the prophets whose words were included in the Old Testament. His prophecies are filled with visions of angels, including one of a trial where a servant of Yahweh was accused by Satan and defended by the Angel of the Lord Himself.[234] Zechariah went on to prophesy that a king would come in humility, riding on a donkey rather than a horse of war. The Messiah would come, speaking peace to the nations and abolish wars among men. His dominion, Zechariah said, would extend not just over Israel, but the entire world.[235]

Over 500 years later, the Messiah was born in Bethlehem; His name was Jesus, a name given to His human mother by the angel Gabriel, who had

---

233   Daniel 10-12
234   Zechariah 3:1ff
235   Zechariah 9:9-10

also appeared to Daniel. While the coming of the Messiah did not abolish war, His words of peace changed its landscape radically. Through Jesus Christ, God now offered reconciliation with Himself to all nations of the earth, not just Israel. Jesus told His followers to love their enemies and pray for blessings on those who oppressed them.[236] Wars among men would continue, but from a spiritual standpoint, the landscape of spiritual warfare was forever changed.

It is the natural inclination of men to view other men as their enemies. After the ascension of Jesus into heaven, Paul of Tarsus would write that the true enemies of followers of God were not human at all. Evil is the result of the devil's schemes, which are implemented by spiritual forces of darkness in the heavenly places.[237] People who do not know God are not the true enemies of those who follow Him; rather, they are unwitting slaves of Satan, held captive by him to do his will.[238] Other human beings are simply hostages and pawns in this cosmic drama.

The true enemies of God and His people are fallen angels, demons dedicated to our destruction.

This truth was clearly illustrated by the earthly life of Jesus Christ. He resisted repeated attempts to make Him the military leader of Israel who would be crowned as earthly king. However, tyrants, both visible and invisible, were dedicated to His destruction. At the beginning of His life, King Herod killed many innocent children in his attempt to destroy young Jesus, a murderous act that was directed by Satan himself.[239] The Pharisees and Sadducees, the ruling classes of the Jewish people, were threatened by Jesus and sought to take His life. They eventually

---

236 Matthew 5:43-48
237 Ephesians 6:10-12
238 2 Timothy 2:26
239 Revelation 12:4

succeeded by exploiting the fears and weaknesses of Herod Antipas and Pontius Pilate, who represented Roman authority in Judea.

When Jesus went into the desert to fast and pray at the beginning of His ministry, He fought not with men, but Satan himself. Jesus consistently identified Satan as the author of the evil that He confronted in Israel. Truth, Jesus told the Pharisees, would set them free from the great demon that held them captive. [240]

In the days when Jesus walked the earth, fallen angels were able to possess, or dwell within, the bodies of men and women. At times, the demons could allow the people they possessed to exhibit powers beyond those of normal human beings.[241] Even many hundreds of these evil spirits could inhabit and afflict a single man.[242] These beings were dedicated to the destruction of the people they dwelled within, often afflicting them with physical disease as well as spiritual torment.[243] They would also cause the people they tormented to do physical harm to themselves.[244]

These dark angels recognized the authority that Jesus Christ had over them during His days in Israel.[245] Later on, they also found that the followers of Jesus could exercise authority over them as well.[246]

Satan, in his efforts to destroy Jesus, would personally possess Judas Iscariot and cause him to betray Jesus.[247] Later that same night, Satan

---

240 John 8:31ff
241 Acts 16
242 Luke 8:30
243 Mark 9:17-18, 9:25
244 Mark 5:5 and Matthew 17:15
245 Luke 8:31
246 Acts 16
247 John 13:26-27

decimated Peter with cowardice and guilt.[248] Perhaps, too, the prince of the power of the air was in the Garden of Gethsemane, causing the anguish that brought sweat like drops of blood to the brow of the Son of God. Jesus had asked His disciples to join His struggle in prayer, but they had neglected to do so. When soldiers arrived to take Him, the apostles reached for their swords, but Jesus told them to put them away. The sword, Jesus told them, was no longer the answer to these conflicts. Just as Jesus declined to rally the swords of men to His defense, He also refused to exercise His authority to summon angels to battle for Him.[249]

Satan, perhaps blinded by his bloodlust, brought about the death of the Messiah. Not long after, he discovered that the cross did not represent his victory, but rather the ultimate triumph of Jesus Christ. His accusations against mankind were rendered void; his guilty power over men was nailed to the cross. Satan was disarmed, defeated and humiliated.[250] Little did he know that God had changed the rules of war, the false ruler of this world did not understand what was happening until it was too late. Had he known, Satan never would have overseen the death of Christ upon the cross.[251]

The death and resurrection of Christ had purchase freedom for all who would trust in Him. Now the mission of His church was to live the life of truth and love that Jesus had modeled for them, thus displaying the incredible wisdom of God to all the spiritual forces in the heavenly places.[252] No longer would God call upon the armies of His people to use physical swords in His service. This did not mean the battle was over, however; Jesus proclaimed that He had not come to bring peace, but a different kind of sword. The new sword is the Truth that is Christ, and

248 Luke 22:31
249 Matthew 26:51ff
250 Colossians 2:14-15
251 1 Corinthians 2:6-8
252 Ephesians 3:10

it does no harm to the bodies of men, but divides the soul from the spirit and judges the intentions of the heart. Those Christian soldiers that follow Christ in this way lose their earthly lives in God's service, but gain eternity.[253]

Years later, on the island of Patmos, John the Apostle had a great vision of heaven and earth. Among the many things he described about the experience is a great battle in heaven, where Satan and his angels wage war with Michael and the angels loyal to God. At the end of the battle, Satan and his angels were thrown down to the earth, and a loud voice in heaven proclaims that salvation and the authority of Christ have come. The defeat of the accuser has been sealed, John writes, by the blood of the Lamb Himself.[254]

Though ultimately defeated, Satan will continue to exert great influence over the earth. In the last days of the earth, Satan and his demons will regain their full powers to afflict mankind when the restrictions of the Pit are removed for a time. Satan will be given the keys to the Pit and he will release his demonic forces to do unprecedented evil upon the earth.[255]

These final days, this *Tribulation*, will be like the days of Noah, Jesus said.[256] In the days of Noah, fallen angels mated with human women and produced hybrid offspring that were mighty in war.[257] In his awesome vision of end times, the apostle John saw a beast, commonly called the Anti-Christ that rises from the Pit in which the demons were held captive.[258] Satan himself waits upon the horizon for the arrival of this beast, who arises to hold great power over the nations. The beast will speak

253 Matthew 10:32-38 and Hebrews 4:12
254 Revelation 12:7-11
255 Revelation 9
256 Luke 16:22-26
257 Genesis 6
258 Revelation 11:7

blasphemies against God and wage war upon those who trust in God. Men and women who do not wear the mark of the beast are not allowed to buy or sell the essentials needed for life.[259] This beast of war may well be the embodiment of a demon, or perhaps the offspring of a fallen angel, or even Satan himself.

The Armageddon seen by John will be the greatest of all battles, when the powers of earth and heaven are in final conflict.[260] After this last period of freedom, Satan, the beast and their followers, humans and demons, will be thrown into the ultimate hell, the lake of fire. Peace will then reign unchallenged upon the earth.[261] The Lord will punish the dark rulers of the earth, both human and angelic, holding them responsible for the evil they brought about throughout history.[262]

In the meantime, the writings of John the Apostle provide additional details of the war in the heavens that continues to impact the world in which we live. Satan, enraged by the turn of affairs, vents his wrath upon mankind, especially followers of the one true God and Jesus Christ.[263] Paul instructs us that our only hope in this battle is to understand and employ spiritual weapons, not earthly ones. The war against dark powers and principalities in the heavens, the true enemies of *all* mankind, is not to be won through physical force. Truth, especially of the good news of Jesus Christ, is our best weapon in the power of the Holy Spirit. Faith, righteous living, prayer and salvation will ultimately defeat the armies of darkness that seek to enslave and destroy all men and women.[264] Truth, Jesus said, sets us free, and makes us children of God instead of children of the father of lies.

---

259 Revelation 13
260 Revelation 16:13ff
261 Revelation 20:7 through Chapter 22
262 Isaiah 24:21-22
263 Revelation Chapter 12
264 Ephesians 6:10ff

Peter followed Jesus Christ for three years before Satan sifted him like wheat and nearly destroyed him. Restored by Jesus Christ, Peter became a bold leader of the early Christians. In one of his letters to other followers of Christ, Peter warned that Satan is constantly prowling like a lion, seeking someone to devour. Be alert, Peter cautioned, and resist the devil. In time, Peter promised, the God of grace will set everything straight; if not in this world, then the next.[265] In the world to come, there will be no more war...and God will wipe every tear from our eyes.[266]

⸺ ∞ ⸺

Scriptures indicate that prayer is one of the primary weapons that followers of Christ are to use in their battle against the true enemy, the spiritual forces of wickedness. The prayer that Jesus taught to His disciples (the Lord's Prayer/Our Father) calls for God's kingdom to come to earth and for His will to be done on earth and in heaven. After requesting forgiveness from God and promising to distribute it to others, the prayer asks God to "lead us not into temptation" and "deliver us from evil."[267] This last phrase is perhaps best translated as "deliver us from the evil *one*." Within this most famous of prayers, Jesus is calling us to be aware of Satan and his evil designs upon our souls.

It has been said that Satan's greatest weapon against followers of God is their reluctance to believe that he even exists. Thus, our prayers are frequently confined to praying for physical healing for ourselves or others. These prayers, while significant, pale in comparison to the importance of the prayers we should be offering for the salvation of others. Our bodies are of great importance to us, but the health of our spirits and souls are far more important.

---

265 1 Peter 5:8-10
266 Revelation 21:4
267 Matthew 6:9-13

Martin Luther, the great reformer, certainly took Satan seriously. He wrote one of the greatest hymns in history in order to warn those who love God of the threat the devil poses to every human being.

A mighty fortress is our God, a bulwark never failing;
our helper He amid the flood of mortal ills prevailing.
For still our ancient foe doth seek to work us woe;
his craft and power are great and armed with cruel hate,
on earth is not his equal.
And though this world, with devils filled
should threaten to undo us,
we will not fear, for God hath willed His
truth to triumph through us.
The Prince of Darkness grim we tremble not for him;
his rage we can endure for lo, his doom is sure;
one little word shall fell him.
"A Mighty Fortress is Our God" by Martin Luther

Whether we acknowledge it or not, every human being is at war. Ignorance of this war will not prevent us from becoming eternal casualties, victims of the invisible forces of darkness around us.

9

Judgment Day

IN THE BEGINNING, God created the heavens and the earth, and declared that all He had created was good. On the day Adam, Eve and Lucifer fell in the Garden of Eden, all of Creation fell with them. Where once all created things had been in complete harmony, now there was strife among the angels, strife between human beings and angels, and many of God's creatures were now separated from Him by their sins of pride. On that fateful day, God promised that a descendant of the woman would eventually rescue the seed of the woman, and crush the head of the serpent, the fallen angel who was the origin of evil itself.

The words of Job are recorded in the book that bears his name. Many consider that book to be the oldest book of Scripture, the first to be set down in writing. In the book, Job states firmly his belief that, at the end of time, his resurrected body will stand before the Lord, and the judgment of the Lord will make all things right. "I know that my Redeemer lives!" Job cried out in the midst of his pain, wishing his words could be preserved forever in stone.[268] Though perhaps not etched in stone, his cry has endured, echoed around the world for over three thousand years.

---

268 Job

The universe, all of Creation, has been longing for the day that things would be set right, which is often called Judgment Day. Believers in Christ have longed for their earthly bodies to be replaced with resurrection bodies for centuries.[269] In heaven itself, the souls of the martyrs have been calling out to God in anticipation of Judgment Day. On that great Day, no more martyrs will be added to their number, for Christ will have come to judge the living and the dead.[270] When will that Day come? No man, no angel knows. Even Christ Himself did not know, at least when He walked the earth as a man. Only God the Father can say when The Day will come.[271]

Many prophets and apostles whose words are recorded in the Old and New Testaments speak of the Day of Judgment, also known as the Day of the Lord. Twenty-five hundred years ago, Daniel prophesied about a great tribulation at the end of time that would be followed by the resurrection of the dead, who would then face judgment. Some would awake to enjoy everlasting life; some would awake to disgrace and everlasting contempt.[272]

In the days of great tribulation, angels will bring great chaos to the earth, wielding the elements of nature as weapons of mass destruction.[273] During this confusion, Satan will bring evil beings to positions of great power upon the earth.[274] The prince of the power of the air will marshal his forces for war in a final attempt to prevent the elimination of his influence over the earth.[275]

---

269 Romans8:22-25

270 Revelation 6:9-11

271 Matthew 24:36

272 Daniel 12:1-2

273 Much of Revelation, e.g. chapter 16

274 Revelation 13

275 Revelation 13:16-17

Jesus Himself spoke of the Day when He would return in power, surrounded by His angels. These angels will first be seen in the skies with
Jesus, surrounded by fire.[276] His *sign,* He said, would appear in the skies
for all to see. Many believe that sign will be the image of the cross which
brought Him victory over the spiritual forces of evil; over Satan and his
fallen angels who have ruled the earth for so long. On Judgment Day, the
powers that be in heaven and on earth will be totally overthrown. Men
who have disregarded God will be in great mourning, and will even cry
out for the mountains to fall upon them in a futile attempt to hide from
the Lord.[277]

The angels of Jesus will gather those faithful to Him from the farthest
ends of heaven and earth. People who have died knowing Jesus Christ
as Savior will then be resurrected from the dead, and join Jesus and His
angels in the air. They will be quickly followed by those who are living
that trust in Christ.[278]

The dead, both the great and the humble, will be gathered before the
throne of Christ. Each of them will be judged according to their deeds.[279]
Those who believe in the Lord's Christ do not need to fear condemna-
tion, but they will be held accountable for their time spent upon the earth
and for their work building the Kingdom of Heaven.[280] Satan and his
angelic minions will be thrown into the lake of fire and they will be
joined by men and women who did not embrace the forgiveness and salvation found only in Christ Himself. Those who truly know Christ will
be distinguished from those who pretend to know Him by their work for
the Kingdom of Heaven through genuine acts of love.[281]

---

276 2 Thessalonians 1:7
277 Luke 23:30
278 1 Thessalonians 4:16-18
279 Revelation 20:12-13
280 1 Corinthians 3:9-15
281 Revelation 20:10, Matthew 25:31ff

When Jesus says that on that Day "the stars will fall from the sky," He is not referring only to distant suns in the universe. He is speaking also of the angelic forces that have governed the operation of the cosmos since the dawn of time. They, too, shall fall. [282] These angels will come under the judgment of human beings who know God and follow His Christ.[283] On the Day of the Lord, the entire structure of the universe will be torn down and rebuilt. Satan will no longer be the ruler of this world. In fact, all fallen angels and their influence will be completely removed from this new reality. Evil will no longer exist on the new earth where God will dwell with His people. Satan and all beings loyal to him will burn in an eternal lake of fire. This fire was designed for fallen angels, but will tragically include misguided human beings as well.[284]

Human beings who know Christ will rise from the dead and dwell within perfected resurrection bodies. Heaven will no longer be separated from the earth; it will descend and merge with our earthly reality.[285] God will dwell on the earth and angels will worship Him side by side with His people.

Nearly two thousand years ago, John the Apostle had a great vision of these final things. He saw angels and humans caught up in the madness of the last days of the earth. At the end of the vision, he saw Jesus, who he followed when He walked the earth. In this vision, John saw Jesus in His glory, as the absolute ruler of the new heaven and earth. Jesus spoke to John declaring Himself to be the beginning and end of all things, and promising that He would soon return to the earth, bringing with Him the angels of God and Judgment Day itself.[286]

---

282   Mark 13:24-27, Matthew 24:29-31, Luke 23:30

283   1 Corinthians 6:3

284   Revelation 20 and 21

285   Revelation 21

286   Revelation 22:12

10

The End

PLEASE ALLOW ME to introduce myself; I'm a being of wealth and taste. At the beginning of time I walked upon the mountain of God as one of the stones of fire. In the Garden of Eden I became the Father of Lies and after the Garden I instructed early man in murder. I became the prince of the power of the air, the ruler of the earth. My lies, so beautifully crafted, lured one-third of the angels, the stars of heaven, to join my activities upon the earth. After an exquisite period of marriage and mayhem, the accursed Michael and his lackeys restricted my brothers and I, confined us to the Pit. Our many children, great and powerful warriors, died in the Flood.

Make no mistake about it; I still called the shots on most of what happened upon the earth. However, it irks me to no end when I find myself serving the purpose of God, which happens all too often.

When the Word became man, I tried to snuff out His life in Bethlehem, but had to settle for the blood of innocent children. Satisfying, to be sure; but it fell far short of the victory I sought. I tempted the Word in the desert, but He rebuked me. I possessed one of His disciples and prompted him to betray Him. I tormented the Word in the Garden of Gethsemane, but He withstood me. I caused men to beat Him, to tear out His beard, to spit upon him, to whip Him and finally to nail His body to a tree. Those exquisite moments were a trick that allowed Him to defeat me, and to damage my power to delude and destroy men and women.

Even when He was dead, He tormented me. He came to the Pit and proclaimed His triumph over me and my brother angels. Then He rose from the dead. Rose from the dead! My greatest weapon was rendered useless by this Son of Man. The seed of the woman whose appearing I had dreaded since the dawn of time.

When He went into heaven, He dragged my brothers and me with Him. Yahweh made every one of us subject to Him. He rules us now. Oh, yes, I can still do damage, but things have changed. When men and women recognize His authority, I lose the chance to destroy them. I can still murder their bodies, and I do so every chance I get. I strike at their loved ones. But ultimately, they are beyond my power to ultimately destroy. When their bodies go, they are with the Word forever. And there is nothing I can do about it.

But every opportunity I get, rest assured I will murder them and send them to their Hero. As long as I am free to do damage, I will. And I will relish every moment of it.

It is written that I will regain my full powers at some point. I will finally be free of this accursed Pit and will be able to do the things I could do before the Flood. I relish the thought and look forward to that day. The Scriptures say these days of freedom won't last long, just a few years. We'll see about that. Once I am out of this place, I will not be easy to corral again. I won't go without a fight.

They say that, once I have had my last shot at the earth, and that my time there will be over. I will be thrown into a lake of fire and tormented. Forever. I won't rule there, as I do in the Pit. I will be a prisoner along with my angels and the foolish humans I have delighted in deceiving.

The very thought of it makes me furious. If and when that Day actually comes, I will have done everything within my powers, which are considerable, to take as many people with me as I can. Humans have seen what I can do in the past, but those things will be as nothing when compared to what I will do at my greatest strength.

I have been pleased to meet you. Hope you have guessed my name. Perhaps now the nature of my game has become clear. If not, all the better. A fool caught by surprise is all the more delicious to destroy.

In the end, we shall have a great deal of time to get acquainted.

11

The Last Word

I AM THE ALPHA.[287]

Before Abraham was, I am.[288]

I am the Word.

In the beginning, I was with God, I was God. I am. All things came into being through Me.[289] I created all things in heaven and on earth. All the angelic forces...the thrones, the dominions, the rulers, the authorities... all of them were created by Me.

I saw Satan fall like lightning.[290]

---

287   Revelation 20:13
288   John 8:58
289   John 1:1-5
290   Luke 10:18

I saw him lie to the children in the Garden. He and the children fell, and the universe groaned in dismay as Satan took control of the earth.[291] My Father gave a promise to the man and woman that their seed, their child, would deliver them from the clutches of the serpent. Satan crawled on his belly and ruled the earth, eventually he lured one third of the angels to join him in his efforts to distort Creation and destroy Our human children.

I am the Seed of the man and the woman, the Son of Man. At the same time, I am the image of the invisible God.[292] I am the exact representation of His nature.[293] For a while, I was made lower than the angels so that I might taste death for every human being.[294] I emptied Myself and took the form of a servant, in the likeness of men. I became like one of My children and lived among them. Many of My children have not understood this.[295]

Angels who were praising God filled the skies after My birth in Bethlehem, but not long after, Satan and a king under his sway slaughtered dozens of innocent children in his first attempt to destroy Me.[296] When I fasted and prayed in the wilderness, he offered to share his twisted authority over the world with Me.[297] Later, he possessed one of My followers and caused him to betray Me.[298] This led to the death of My body, which was given up for you.[299] Satan had orchestrated My death, but to his surprise this did

---

291 Romans 8:22
292 Colossians 1:15-16
293 Hebrews 1:3
294 Hebrews 2:9
295 John 1
296 Matthew 2:16 and Revelation 12:4
297 Luke 4:5-6
298 John 13:27
299 Luke 22:19

not bring him his greatest victory. My cross brought ultimate, humiliating defeat for him and the angels who serve him.[300]

After I died on the cross and rose from the dead, an angel sat at the entrance to My empty tomb and proclaimed that I had risen.[301] As I ascended to heaven, I was exalted by My Father over every spiritual being in Creation. The knee of every angel, those in heaven, on earth and under the earth, now bows to me.[302]

The story of the Son of Man is good news for all men, for all of Creation. This story is one that the angels themselves longed for centuries to witness.[303] Men and women who have chosen to embrace Me are now charged with telling the story to others; the tale is told with their lives, not merely their words. In this way, they glorify Me and My Father.[304] They demonstrate the infinite facets of My Father's wisdom to the entire universe, to the angelic powers and principalities who reign over Creation as My deputies.[305] The purpose of My church is to make My Father's wisdom known to all thinking beings, to every angel and every man, even as I prepare a place for Our children with Us in heaven.[306]

Every person who seeks shall find Us.[307] My Spirit will guide all who seek Me into truth, and will speak all the true things that the Father has entrusted to Me.[308] The invisible powers that rule the cosmos, the

---

300 Colossians 2:14-15
301 Mark 16:4-6
302 Philippians 2:7-10
303 1 Peter 1:12 and Ephesians 3:8ff
304 Matthew 5:15
305 Ephesians 3:8-12
306 John 14:2
307 Jeremiah 29:13 and Matthew 7:7 among others
308 John 16:12ff

thrones, principalities and the dark rulers cannot separate you from My Father's love for you, which is manifested in Me.[309]

I will return to the earth in the skies, in the same fashion I left it. My angels told My disciples this on the day I ascended.[310] I will come again to judge the living and the dead, and of My kingdom there will be no end. I will come in glory with My angels, and they will sort out everything and everyone who is evil.[311] The world will be perfect, and My Father will wipe every tear from human eyes.[312]

I stand at your doorway and knock. Answer the door, and I will dine with you.[313] It is not My Father's will that any man or woman should perish.[314] He has shown Us to every single person ever born through the wonder of the worlds We created.[315] I entered that Creation, I became man to be a friend to sinners.[316] I have laid down My life for My friends.[317] If you do not know Me, you are held captive by Satan himself.[318] I have come to set you free.[319] My purpose in life is to do My Father's will. If you will join Me in that mission, you will remain My friend for eternity.[320]

Join Me in My death, and you will join Me in life forever.[321] Because of what Satan led your ancestors to do in the Garden, all men and women

309   Romans 8:37-39
310   Acts 1:9-11
311   Matthew 13:41
312   Revelation 21:3-4
313   Revelation 3:20
314   Matthew 18:14
315   Romans 1:20
316   Matthew 11:19
317   John 15:13
318   2 Timothy 2:26
319   John 8:36
320   John 15:14
321   Romans 6:4

must die once. The tragic reality is that those who do not accept My offer of friendship shall die twice, and the second death will last forever.[322] Be earnest and repent. I am the door. Knock, and all will be open to you.[323]

Those men and women who have acknowledged Me before others will be acknowledged by Me before My angels.[324] I will reward each person for what they have done.[325] Each time they showed kindness toward people in distress, it was as if they had done it for Me.[326]

The men and women who have followed Me faithfully shall then turn and judge the angels themselves.[327] The devil that has deceived so many for so long will be thrown into the lake of fire and brimstone. He and the angels loyal to him will be tormented there, forever.[328] Though it grieves Me deeply, many men and women will join them because their names will not appear in My book of life.[329]

This lake of fire was not intended for you, not designed for you, but for Satan and his angels.[330] Life and death are set before you this day. Choose life.[331]

When the Day of Judgment comes to an end, My Father will make all things new. His throne and My throne shall be in the great heavenly city,

---

322 Revelation 20:6 and 21:8
323 Matthew 7:7
324 Luke 12:8
325 Matthew 16:27
326 Matthew 25:40
327 1 Corinthians 6:3
328 Revelation 20:10
329 Revelation 20:15
330 Matthew 25:41
331 Deuteronomy 30:19

and Our Spirit will be before those thrones.[332] Those men and angels who have been faithful to Us will dwell with Us there forever.[333]

I am coming soon.

I am the Word.

I am the Omega.[334]

332 Revelation 4:5
333 Revelation 22:3-5
334 Revelation 22:12-13

Afterthoughts

A COUPLE OF YEARS ago, when I was on the verge of completing my research into what the Bible says about angels, there was a tremendous thunderstorm near our home. At the time, when we sat on our back steps, we had a beautiful view of open fields with woods in the distance. It was not raining at our house yet, but miles away, the heavens were putting on a fantastic light show. As I sat on my back steps, lightning was flashing across the sky dozens of times every minute among majestic clouds, and thunder rumbled in symphony with the display.

Ordinarily, when watching a storm like this one, TV meteorologists would come to my mind, with their scientific predictions and descriptions of the weather. Not this night, though. I was thinking about the fact that the Bible says that angels, under God's watchful eye, were putting on the light show in the sky. Even now, years later, that night comes to mind almost every time I teach about what the Bible has to say about angels.

Why? Because what I have learned about angels has totally changed the way I look at the world. Spiritual beings are busy all around us. They influence our weather. They cause natural disasters. They rescue people in the midst of those disasters. They whisper guidance, both good and evil, to kings, presidents, and peasants. They are watching us. Some are helping us. Some are dedicated to our destruction. They move the hearts of individuals and they influence the destinies of nations.

Whether these powerful beings love God or hate Him, they all serve Him.
They fight with each other. Some fight with us. Some fight for us. What these
beings do affects every person on the face of the earth every day.

As a result, I feel as if I no longer live in a world dominated by science. Rather,
I feel like I am in the middle of a tale from Greek mythology. And in a way,
I am. So are you. The epic story that the Bible tells is still in progress. We are
all players on a supernatural stage.

Over the last twenty centuries, especially the last two, the world view of people who claim Jesus Christ as their Savior has dramatically shifted. This process shifted into fast forward in 1859 when Charles Darwin published The
Origin of the Species and put forth evolution as the alternative explanation for
how human beings came about on the earth. At last, human beings could
latch onto a creation story that didn't seem so primitive. This new worldview
dovetailed so nicely with science, which was making the most rapid advances
in human history. Those who treasured science above all else had a way to
explain the world that did not seem like something from a fairy tale.

As evolution increasingly became the "spectacles" through which many
viewed the world, those who clung to Creation as described in the Bible were
seen as primitive and uneducated. Schools (especially universities) embraced
Darwin's views and philosophies that emerged from them. Law schools
applied those philosophies and Bibles were no longer respected resources
in court rooms, even though our common law (and that of Britain, from
whence it came) was based upon it. Books, magazines, movies and newspa-
pers increasingly ridiculed people with traditional Bible beliefs. They were
labeled "fundamentalists" and were portrayed as the villains in the story of
scientific progress.

To an extent, the abrasive response of the Church assisted the process of
marginalizing anyone who viewed the Bible as literal truth. The mainstream
media eagerly has eagerly leaped forth to highlight the un-Christian behavior

of Christians whenever possible. And, unfortunately, it hasn't been too hard to find examples of Bible-believing folks behaving badly.

Some folks have sought to merge the two worldviews, blending evolutionary science with the Bible. Belief in evolution makes them seem more rational and approachable; belief that God is in charge of the evolutionary process keeps God in charge of the universe. There are many people who truly know and love God who hold this viewpoint.

Regardless of where you stand on this issue, I invite you to consider the impact that the elevation of science over Scripture has had on the views and philosophies of our culture. In response to this pressure, churches have increasingly "demythologized" the Bible. Miracles are explained away or omitted from discussion completely. Sunday sermons focus primarily on Paul's epistles and neglect the powerful stories of Biblical history. Some sermons skim only the Bible's surface, and are about self-help, encouragement and earthly prosperity and happiness. The knowledge about Biblical history and events held by people in the pews has become increasingly shallow.

Angels? Demons? Satan? Heaven? Hell? They just don't belong in this scenario. That's why they are rarely discussed in church. Angels are confined to watching over the manger, and little else.

While Christians should never be obsessed with angels, nor worship them, nor pray to them, to ignore them is foolish. If the Bible is true (and it is) then it is important that we understand that the activities of angels and demons affect us on a daily basis. Our lack of understanding in this area makes us increasingly vulnerable to the attacks of invisible spiritual forces that work constantly to defeat the cause of Christ.

The world described by the Bible is surrounded by spiritual beings and forces not visible to us. Science helps explain what we see, but it does not adequately capture the reality we sense in our hearts. We instinctively know there is something more than what we see, and the Bible tells us what that something is.

According to Scripture, the essence of faith is belief in the unseen. (Hebrews 11:1ff) If we dismiss the unseen things described in Scripture as irrelevant to our lives in this world, we have missed a very important boat.

Up until a couple of centuries ago, theology (the study of God) was considered to be "the queen of sciences."

Theology remains the queen of sciences, whether we recognize it or not. It is not to be segregated from our daily lives, or confined within the four walls of our church.

I hope the information in this book has impacted your view of the world as it has mine.

There are storms all around us. Some we see in the skies. Some we see on TV. Some we see in our society and in our families.

God whispered to Job in the midst of a storm. He speaks to us in the midst of storms as well. The instruments He often uses to do so are the voices of angels. They remain His messengers, even today.

It is the reason for their existence.

Are we listening?

He who has ears, let him hear.

Coming soon: more
about the angels

You just finished ready the story of the angels as told by the Bible. No doubt this raised many questions in your mind about angels and demons. Perhaps you are pondering:

What do angels look like?
Do they have wings?
What are some of the many forms angels can take?
What are the different kinds of angels?
Are there guardian angels?
Are angels involved in natural disasters?
What is the relationship between angels and the members of the Trinity?
Do we become angels when we die?
What happens to us between the time we die and the time when we are resurrected?
What do we know about heaven and hell?

These and many other questions are addressed in

Angels: Our Strange Neighbors
by Ron Wenzel

This comprehensive examination of everything the Bible has to say about angels, both good and evil, should be available (Lord willing) by the end of 2015 or early 2016.

Made in the USA
Middletown, DE
15 September 2015